The Boa Constrictor Manual

FROM THE EXPERTS AT
ADVANCED VIVARIUM SYSTEMS™

By Philippe de Vosjoli, Roger Klingenberg, DVM,
and Jeff Ronne

THE HERPETOCULTURAL LIBRARY™
Advanced Vivarium Systems™
Irvine, California

Karla Austin, *Business Operations Manager*
Nick Clemente, *Special Consultant*
Jarelle S. Stein, *Editor*
Jill Dupont, *Production*
Kendra Strey, *Assistant Editor*
Cover and layout design by Michael Capozzi

All photos by Philippe de Vosjoli except where otherwise indicated.
The additional photographs in this book are courtesy of David Barker,
pp. 13, 19, 34, 58, 59; Patrick Briggs, pp. 45, 51; Jeff Gee, pp. 10, 18;
Tom Greek, p 28; Kevin & Sue Hanley, p. 7; Pete Kahl, pp. 8, 55; Roger
Klingenberg, pp. 57-58, 77-78, 82, 84-93; Zig Lescszysnki, pp. 5, 53;
Bill Love, pp. 14, 16, 32, 50; John Mack, p. 55; Tim Mead, p. 11; G & C
Merker, pp. 21, 45; Dan Nedrelo, p. 43; Michael Novy, pp. 37, 55; Jeff
Ronne, pp. 9, 12, 15, 52; Brian Sharp, p. 33; Rick Staub, pp. 30, 40, 41,
72, 74; A. St. Pierre, pp. 17, 25; John Tyson, p. 42.

LCCN: 96-183295
ISBN: 1-882770-76-5

AVS ADVANCED VIVARIUM SYSTEMS™

An Imprint of BowTie Press®
A Division of BowTie, Inc.
3 Burroughs
Irvine, CA 92618
www.avsbooks.com
1-866-888-5526

We want to hear from you. What books would you like to see in the
future? Please feel free to write us with any comments on our AVS
books.

Printed in Singapore
10 9 8 7 6 5 4 3 2 1

CONTENTS

ACKNOWLEDGEMENTS

Special thanks to all of the boa breeders, photographers and good friends who supplied the photos and information that made this book possible, including David and Tracy Barker, Patrick Briggs, Bill Love, Jeff Gee, Steve Hammond, Kevin and Sue Hanley, Rich Ihle, Pete Kahl, Lloyd Lemke, John Mack, Tim Mead, Jeff Ronne, Brian Sharp, Ron and A. St. Pierre, and Terry Vandeventer.

INTRODUCTION

Although herpetoculture, the keeping of reptiles and amphibians, has undergone tremendous changes during the last twenty years, boa constrictors have remained the most popular large snake kept by the general public. Their continuing popularity is well deserved, and speaks very highly for the species. They are beautiful, hardy, and, for the most part, docile and safe pets. Today, "boaculture" has also come a long way from basic pet ownership, and the field bustles with creativity and excitement. Skilled breeders now breed these beautiful snakes in a great variety of "flavors," from subspecies and locality variants to designer patterns and color morphs. In the truest sense, the snakes have been transformed into living works of art.

As a consequence of the large number of boa constrictors imported, kept, bred, sold, and traded, veterinarians and keepers have identified a variety of diseases and problems common to boas. One viral disease known as IBD (inclusion body disease), often called boa AIDS, shocked the herp world by showing that an epidemic disease could wipe out a significant percentage of these animals in captivity, and demands immediate attention by all those involved with boas and pythons. As I assembled the material for this book, it was clear that I needed a qualified veterinarian to address these critical health issues, and I asked my good friend and herp vet extraordinaire Roger Klingenberg to join me in writing this manual. He came to the rescue, as he has done on several other occasions, and compiled a disease section that is as thorough as it is practical.

The material regarding the captive breeding of boa constrictors also needed major updates. Although I have kept and bred boa constrictors, I have focused on husbandry and, more recently, categorization of boa constrictor varieties and morphs. To provide high-quality captive-breeding information, I had to find a boa specialist. I had read a piece by Jeff Ronne on breeding boa constrictors in Reptiles magazine and had been very impressed by his detailed records and acute observations. I called Jeff and asked if he would be interested in writing a chapter for this book and, as luck would have it, he graciously accepted; never has boa constrictor breeding been reported in such detail. If you have any questions about boa breeding, his interesting chapter, rich with details from lengthy observation, will certainly provide the answers.

In other words, a lot of work went into compiling the information for what was supposed to be a simple revision of my original book. But now, the primary goal of the project—a thorough introduction to keeping and breeding boas—has been accomplished. However, after spending countless hours examining hundreds of boa constrictors, experimenting with various setups, and exchanging ideas with boa hobbyists, I've realized there is still much more work to be done with this species. Herpetologists need to identify wild populations, study the ecology of these populations recognize the many herpetocultural morphs, research the genetics of the species, and establish a registry system. The list goes on. Suffice it to say that the future of boa keeping promises to be more exciting than one could ever imagine.

The Colombian boa constrictor is one of the most popular species of large snakes.

CHAPTER 1

GENERAL INFORMATION

B oa constrictors are members of the subfamily Boinae in the family Boidae. Like pythons, boas are primitive snakes that have vestigial remnants of the pelvis and hind limbs of their lizard-like ancestors. The cloacal spurs on the sides of the vent, external features that are well developed in male boa constrictors, are connected to these vestigial hind limbs.

Boa constrictors are large snakes with a wide distribution, ranging south from Mexico, through central America and South America, to Argentina. In contrast to pythons, which are egg laying, all boas give birth to live young.

Other Boas

For a long time, boa constrictors were considered monotypic, meaning that they were the only species in the genus Boa, but a recent publication by Kluge suggests that the two species of Malagasy ground boas (*Acrantophis dumerili* and *A. madagascariensis*) should be included in the genus Boa along with the Malagasy tree boa (The species *Sanzinia madagascariensis* would

A hypomelanistic, "Salmon" phase common boa constrictor. The line was developed by Rich Ihle.

become *Boa mandrita*). If this seems outrageous to some, I recommend that they first read Kluge's ground-breaking paper and the careful methodology he has applied to reach these conclusions.

Scientific Name

To avoid the confusion often caused by common names, most hobbyists use scientific names when referring to amphibians and reptiles. On the bright side, virtually all boa constrictor owners already know the scientific name of the boa constrictor. It is one of the few cases where the common and scientific names are the same: *Boa constrictor*.

Taxonomy

The number of types of boa constrictors depends on the system of categorization and on the criteria established for recognizing differences. Herpetologists, typically individuals with university training in herpetology, currently recognize one species and between six to ten subspecies. The six species recognized by all herpetologists are:

- Common boa constrictor (*Boa constrictor imperator*)
- Red-tailed boa constrictor (*B. c. constrictor*)
- Clouded boa constrictor (*B. c. nebulosus*)
- San Lucia boa constrictor (*B. c. orophias*)
- Short-tailed boa constrictor (*B. c. amarali*)
- Argentine boa constrictor (*B. c. occidentalis*)

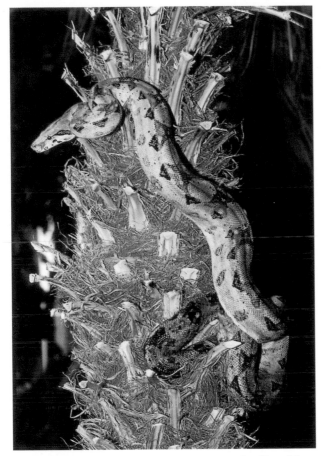

A rare morph of the Crawl Cay common boa constrictor, found on an island off of Belize. It has inconspicuous and reduced tail blotches, and is capable of significant color change. The owner, Tim Mead, reported a litter of twelve from this form.

The following four species are not recognized by all herpetologists:

- Northwest Peruvian boa constrictor (*B. c. ortonii*)
- Peruvian black-tailed boa constrictor (*B. c. longicauda*)
- Ecuadoran black-bellied boa constrictor (*B. c. melanogaster*)
- Saboga Island boa constrictor (*B. c. sabogae*)

Protection

All pythons and boas, including boa constrictors, are considered vulnerable by the Convention on the International Trade in Endangered Species (CITES) and listed under Appendix II. This means that those who wish to internationally import or export the animals need special permits. The Argentine boa constrictor is currently listed as endangered by CITES under Appendix I, which means they cannot be exported from Argentina and Paraguay, and that owners require special permits to move captive-bred and long-term captives between countries.

Size

Newborn boa constrictors range from 14 to 22 inches in length and weigh between 2 and 3 ounces. Neonate Colombian boa constrictors are typically around 18 inches in length. Neonate red-tailed boas from Guyana, Surinam, and the Peruvian Amazon basin tend to be larger. The adult size for Colombian boa constrictors is 4 to 9 feet, with occasional specimens reaching or exceeding 11 feet. Adult Hog Island boas (*B. c. imperator,* Hog Island) typically range from 3 to 5 feet. The largest boa constrictor is the true red-tailed boa (*B. c. constrictor*) from the Amazon basin of South America, which reaches 12 feet in length. Rare specimens reach up to 14 feet in length. On the other hand, there are areas in the true red-tailed boas range of where the

This common boa is double heterozygous for "Ghost" (a cross between hypomelanistic and anerythristic specimens).

length of adults typically ranges from 4 to 7 feet. The largest boa constrictor on record was red-tail from Trinidad said to have been more than 18 feet long. However, this rumor has been disproved, and researchers think the maximum size for a boa constrictor is probably around 14 feet.

Relatively few boa constrictors raised in captivity exceed a weight of 60 pounds, and many of the Colombian boa constrictors and other forms of Boa constrictor imperator do not exceed 30 pounds as adults. I examined a large, healthy female Colombian boa constrictor that measured 10 feet 8 inches and weighed 48 pounds.

Longevity

Boa constrictors are among the longest lived snake species. Reports of boa constrictors living for twenty years or more are fairly common. The oldest specimen on record lived for forty years, three months, and fourteen days at the Philadelphia Zoological Gardens.

Adult boa constrictor *longicauda*.

Sexing

The easiest way to sex newborn boa constrictors is to attempt to manually evert its hemipenes, which only appear in males. To perform this method, hold the newborn boas so that the hind part of its body is positioned belly side up within your hand. Use your thumb to hold the area just in front of the vent (the opening to the cloaca) against your index finger. Allow the base of the tail (located just past the vent) to rest on your index finger. Then, using a gentle rolling motion and starting at an area about two thirds of an inch past the vent, roll your other thumb toward the vent while applying pressure. If done correctly, this will cause a male boa to evert its hemipenes. If you are not familiar with this process, have an experienced individual demonstrate it for you. Inexperienced keepers can easily injure their snakes by applying too much pressure.

To be sure that you properly sexed your snakes, have your (probable) female boas probed with a 1 mm sexing probe. The probe will reach a depth of two to four subcaudal scales in females, seven to eight subcaudal scales in neonate males, and ten to twelve subcaudal scales in adult males.

Probing is the only way to positively sex adult boa constrictors, but several characteristics, such as the larger body size of females, larger spurs to the sides of the vent in males, and broader thicker tails in males, provide relatively reliable clues to their gender. Breeding behaviors are also very good indicators of the sex of your snakes.

Probing adult boa constrictors is a two-person operation. One individual has to control the snake being probed and firmly hold the vent area of the snake toward the individual performing the probing (belly side up). To help con-

A short-tailed boa constrictor.

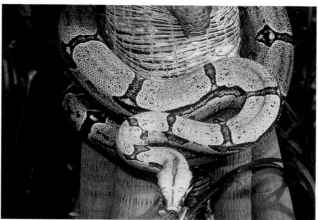

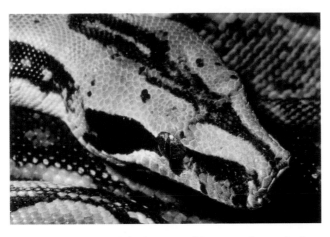

An Argentine black-tailed boa.

trol large snakes and facilitate probing, put the snake in a cloth snake bag, allowing only the tail to remain outside. For adult boa constrictors, use 2 to 4 mm probes, depending on the size of the snakes.

To probe a boa constrictor, hold the area just in front of the vent with one hand, and use your thumb to pull back the area in front (towards the head) of the anal scale to expose the cloacal opening. After moistening the probe with clean water, gently insert the probe into one of two small openings visible to the side of the cloacal opening with your other hand; use a slight twirling motion. In adult females, the probe will enter a musk gland to a length of two to four subcaudal scales, while in adult males, it will enter an inverted hemipenis to a length of ten to twelve subcaudal scales. To verify a reading, repeat the process on the other side. This is a procedure is best performed and taught by experienced individuals. Most specialized reptile dealers will perform this service when you intend to buy animals of specific sexes.

Diet and Growth

It is difficult to present a typical growth pattern for boa constrictors, because their growth rate is affected by their sub species, population characteristics, individual characteristics, the temperature of their enclosure, and their feeding regimen. In addition, published information on this

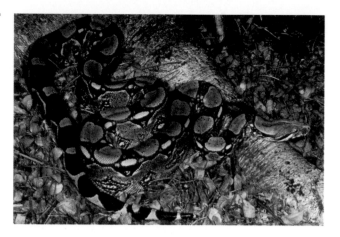

The popular Colombian boa constrictor originated west of the Andes. Most specimens in the pet trade were collected from an area known as the Magdalena River Valley, and shipped out of Baranquilla.

subject is of marginal value because species are frequently misnamed or improperly categorized.

In a very broad sense, the growth pattern demonstrated by Colombian boas and red-tailed boas is as follows:

From newborn to twelve months: Most specimens grow 3 to 4 feet in length, though some Colombian boa constrictors can grow to nearly 5 feet, and a few individuals reach almost 6 feet during that period of time.

From twelve to twenty-four months: Typical specimens range from to 4 to 7 feet in length, though some reach a length of 8 feet, and some individuals occasionally reach nearly 9 feet. As a general rule, *B. c. imperator* from Colombia are the fastest growing boa constrictors. True red-tailed boas tend to grow at a somewhat slower pace, and Argentine boa constrictors grow even slower than them.

On an optimal feeding schedule, the relative growth rate of most boa constrictors significantly decreases after twenty-four months. Typically, after twenty-four months the relative annual growth rate decreases to 10–20 percent of the animals current size (in contrast to 100–300 percent during the first year), and continues to decrease as the animal becomes older.

By keeping boa constrictors in temperatures at the low end of their requirements (80–82° Fahrenheit), and by feeding them a moderate-sized prey item every two weeks as babies or every two to three weeks as adults, it is possible to stunt their growth so that males do not exceed 5 feet and females do not exceed 7 feet (Colombian boas and red-tailed boas). As long as your snake maintains a decent weight, this dietary "stunting" will not harm its health (see Breeding).

Notes On Common Species

Common Boa Constrictor (*B. c. imperator,* Daudin, 1803)

Distribution
Common boa constrictors are found from the northern Mexican states Sonora and Tamaulipas, through Central America and Colombia, south through western Ecuador and northwestern Peru. Boa c. imperator populations are separated from B. c. constrictor populations by the Andes.

Characteristics
Common boas have less than 253 ventral scales, and the mid-body scale count ranges from fifty-five to seventy-nine. They also have twenty-one or more dorsal blotches (between the neck and vent). Colombian boa constrictors have higher scale counts. The belly is not speckled or lightly speckled in most specimens, and the ventral pattern of the posterior body and tail is faint or smudged.

A common boa constrictor.

15

Red-Tailed Boa Constrictor (*B. c. constrictor*, Lanais, 1768)

Distribution
These South American boas are found east of the Andes. Their range includes eastern Ecuador, northern and eastern Peru, northern Bolivia, some of Brazil, central and eastern Colombia, Venezuela, the Guinas, Trinidad, and Tobago.

Characteristics
Red-tailed boas have less than twenty blotches between the neck and above the vent. They have 234 to 250 ventral scales, and eighty-nine to ninety-five mid-body scale rows. Their bellies are usually speckled in black, though more so toward the posterior body, and they have defined red blotches on the ventral surface of their posterior body and tail. They are the largest subspecies of boa constrictor, and rank among the most beautiful.

Short-tailed Boa Constrictor (*B. c. amarali*, Stull 1932)

Distribution:
Brazil and Bolivia

Characteristics
Short-tailed boas have 226 to 237 ventral scales, and twenty-

A wild Peruvian red-tailed boa. Arguably one of the most beautiful boa constrictors, Peruvian red-tailed boas' background coloration often has a strong yellowish tint, and bright red posterior body and tail blotches.

two dorsal blotches between the neck and vent. Females grow up to 7 feet, but are typically smaller. Their tails are relatively short. When viewed from the side, a short-tailed boa's head looks more flattened than in other boa constrictors. Their background coloration ranges from gray and silver to a rich, dusky yellow. They have heavily speckled, dark bellies.

Peruvian Black-Tailed Boas (*B. c. longicauda,* Price and Russo, 1993)

Distribution
Original specimens were said to hail from near Tumbes, in northern Peru.

Characteristics
The validity of this subspecies is in question, with some herpetologists claiming that it is actually *B. c. ortonii,* and others claiming that it is simply a southern morph of *B. c. imperator.* Whatever the case, it is a distinct morph with a wide, central head stripe, and black anterior and posterior face markings. It has dark, often interconnected saddles, and its background color ranges from yellowish brown to a light powder-gray, usually with extensive amounts of black. The posterior body and tail blotches are black. Relatively few specimens exist in herpetoculture.

Anerythristic Colombian common boa constrictor.

Argentine Boa Constrictor (*Boa constrictor occidentlis*, Philippi 1873)

Distribution
Argentine boa constrictors are found in Argentina and Paraguay, between the Andes and the Prana River south to the provinces of Cordoba, San Luiz, and Mendoza.

Characteristics
Argentine boas have between 242 and 251 ventral scales and 29 or 30 interconnected dorsal blotches. The nicest specimens are mostly black with lacy white peppering. Adult females range between 7 and 9 feet.

The beautiful "Blood" phase common boa was developed by Ron St. Pierre.

An Argentine black-tailed boa.

CHAPTER 2

BEFORE YOU BUY

Boas are beautiful, wonderful snakes and among the most desirable of the large snakes species, but is a boa constrictor what you really want?

Many first-time buyers fail to understand that the "cute, little snake" that they purchased will eventually grow into a huge animal that will require both arms and hands for handling. The once adorable boa will also outgrow its small enclosure and may one day require a custom-built enclosure that takes up as much room as a large piece of furniture. Most first-time boa owners also tend to overlook their snake's growing feeding requirements; a baby snake that begins feeding on small mice may eventually require prey the size of a large rabbit.

If you want a large snake, there are other boid species, such as rainbow boas (*Epicrates cenchria*), that don't grow quite as large and are easier to manage as adults. Yet, boa constrictors also have great qualities: large and impressive size, beauty, and often (when captive-raised from juveniles and regularly handled) a docile and consistent disposition. But is a large snake really what you want?

The decision is similar to that which confronts a dog buyer. Before purchasing a snake, you must consider your lifestyle. Do you live in an apartment or a large home? Do you have children? How much free time do you have? Can you easily obtain the necessary food items for your pet? Will space or heating be a problem? Is the boa constrictor going to end up in your studio apartment or in a special room on the bottom floor of the house? Are your young children likely to tamper with it? Will you have the time to take proper care of your snake? Consider all pertinent questions before purchasing a boa constrictor.

If you decide that you really want a large snake, and that

you can properly care for it, none are a better choice than the boa constrictor. A boa never reaches the problematic large size and weight of Burmese pythons and reticulated pythons, and compared to many other animals, boas are relatively safe pets when maintained and handled in a responsible manner.

Responsible Herpetoculture

Every year there are a number of newsworthy incidents involving escaped boa constrictors or people displaying their snakes in public. In 1997, a boa constrictor found in Los Angeles eating a woman's pet chihuahua generated an unusual amount of bad press. This incident led to regulatory proposals and public hearings on peoples' right to keep snakes as well as their rights to be spared exposure to snakes. In Fillmore, California, an escaped snake found on the mayor's porch led to a ban on snake ownership. These incidents threaten our right to keep boa constrictors and the future of the herpetocultural hobby. Preventing such incidents is relatively simple and should be a primary consideration of every snake keeper and dealer.

Active Prevention

To help prevent further incidents, dealers should require that prospective buyers purchase, or demonstrate that they own, a secure cage before selling a boa constrictor. Buyers

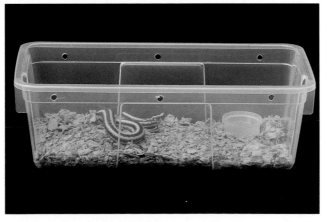

Research a snake's requirements before purchasing it. This is a temporary basic setup, most setup environments would also include decorative branches, shelter, and heat source.

should purchase or build cages with a secure locking mechanism before purchasing a large snake. Owners should never allow their snakes to roam free in their home and should not keep them in makeshift enclosures.

Experts further recommend that all keepers of large snakes adopt the American Federation of Herpetoculture (AFH) guidelines for the responsible keeping of large constrictors. While the AHF no longer exists, the following guidelines remain valid:

- In consideration of the right of the general public not to be exposed unexpectedly to snakes such as large constrictors and in consideration of the irresponsible behavior of certain snake owners, the AFH recommends regulations whereby snakes should not be allowed to be openly displayed in a public setting outside of proper and established forums for such practices such as pet establishments, herpetological shows, educational displays and presentations, and other special displays whereby members of the public are forewarned that a snake(s) will be displayed in the open.

- The AFH recommends that all snakes be transported in a manner that precludes escape: In a sturdy cloth bag free of holes or tears which is then placed inside a box or similar container with holes for aeration. The box or container should then be sealed or locked shut. Another alternative is to double bag snakes. Care must be taken to use sturdy cloth bags with a weave that allows for adequate air flow. Airlines should be consulted as to their requirements when shipping snakes by air.

- For the keeping of large constrictors 8 feet or more, the AFH recommends general caging regulations whose effects are similar to those which require dog owners to keep their pets within the confines of their property. Caging regulations for large snakes should require owners of such snakes to house them in secure cages with hinged top or doors, or a sliding glass front, which include a locking mechanism. Such enclosures should preferably be contained in a large room modified to prevent snake escapes and with a door which shall be kept shut or locked when the room is not occupied by the owners. This recommendation is made to require responsible herpetocultural practices by individuals with consideration for the animals, for family members and for members of the general public. As herpetoculturists, we will all benefit by adopting these responsible practices.

- When handling any of the giant snakes (green anaconda, Indian and Burmese python, African rock python, reticulated python and amethystine python) over 8 feet, the AFH recommends that another individual be present or, at the very least, be within calling distance. The probability of any serious problem occurring when handling such snakes is very remote but the AFH position is that herpetoculturists, out of responsibility to themselves, to family members and to other herpetoculturists, should handle and maintain large snakes in a manner that significantly prevents the likelihood of any accident or incident.

- The AFH does not recommend the ownership of the above-mentioned giant constrictors as well as other large (adult size over 7 feet) boid snakes by minors without parental consent to assume responsibility for proper housing, maintenance, and supervision when handling.

- As with any other animals such as dogs, owners of large constrictors should remember that they can be liable for the medical costs of treating injuries as well as additional financial damages for traumas or damage caused by their animals.

Regulations

Recently, many city and state officials have drafted ordinances to control or restrict ownership of large snakes. Various agencies and organizations directly or indirectly support these regulations, particularly with regards to the ownership of large constrictors (typically boas and pythons that reach an adult length of more than 8 feet). They contend that the public should be protected from the remote possibility of danger from these animals. Most of these proposed regulations conceal the underlying bias against snakes that permeates most people's attitudes towards reptiles.

After examining these regulations, one would assume that potentially dangerous animals should not, as a matter of course, be possessed by the general public. One might also be led to believe that these various agencies look out for our welfare. In fact, numerous animals condoned by these agencies and the federal government present far greater probabilities of danger than those presented by large constrictors. Dogs raised and kept by irresponsible owners can be extremely dangerous, a fact well supported by statistical data (ten to fifteen Americans die each year because of dog attacks, and millions of dollars are spent treating dog bites). Cats scratch and bite (their bites account for a significant percentage of the animal-related injuries reported each year), and they can carry some dangerous diseases. Even human beings seem to be more dangerous than snakes; In fact, based on available statistics, a human being has a far greater chance of being seriously injured by a bite from a fellow human than by a large constrictor.

Despite the numerous potential dangers posed by other pets, poorly informed and biased state and local agencies regularly propose laws and ordinances that ban ownership of large constrictors. If one relied on hard data rather than prejudice, one could make a much better case for banning ownership of dogs, horses, guns, or automobiles.

Boa constrictors have virtually no significant behavioral propensity to kill humans by constriction, and to date, I have been unable to find a single authenticated report of a human being killed by a boa constrictor. Though various rumors abound, the facts are often distorted and exaggerated, and the snakes are often misidentified.

Considering the safety record of the several hundred thousand boa constrictors imported and sold in the United States over the last twenty-five years, and considering the much more threatening risks generally accepted as a normal part of everyday life, large constrictors present very little real danger. One can only assert that boa constrictors, warrant caution and common sense when handling.

The Law

Before purchasing a boa or any other large constrictor, check your state, county, and local regulations for provisions applying to the ownership of reptiles by individuals. In addition to contacting the agencies in charge of implementing these regulations, you can get pertinent information from local herpetological societies. It does not pay to break the law; before you know it, you could be making newspaper headlines and the six o'clock news. If local authorities call in state or federal enforcement agencies (such as the State Fish and Game and U.S. Fish and Wildlife Departments) to investigate the possibility of other infractions, you may experience violations of your privacy that you are not likely to forget. In some areas, possible possession of an illegal reptile gets more media attention than a major drug bust.

Inclusion Body Disease (IBD)

Until now, herpetoculturists have not faced deadly epidemics capable of wiping out large numbers of certain reptiles. In herpetoculture, the first disease with epidemic potential was IBD, a viral disease that affects boa constrictors and other boid snakes. Because the signs of the disease may not become apparent for months or years, IBD has

A blotch-free Central American common boa, originally from El Salvador.

spread through captive boa constrictor populations at an alarming rate. It is usually fatal. Like acquired immunodeficiency syndrome (AIDS), IBD is caused by a retrovirus, and like AIDS, the retrovirus is spread by an exchange of bodily fluids from an infected specimen. Mites, ingestion of fecal material, and copulation can all spread this viral disease. In addition, if a female boa was infected before or during pregnancy, its babies will also be infected.

One of the major problems with IBD is that there is no simple test for diagnosis; apparently healthy boa constrictors can carry the disease for months or years before they show any signs of illness.

Quarantine

To prevent the spread of IBD and other diseases, isolate all new specimens from each other and your existing collection, and eliminate any mites or other parasites, which act as a vector for the spread of disease. A general rule of herpetoculture is to always care for quarantined animals after caring for your established collection to reduce the risk of spreading disease.

Using disposable paper towels, which also make an excellent temporary substrate, regularly clean and disinfect the cages of quarantined animals. Do not move water bowls between cages and make sure to clean and disinfect each bowl separately. Wash your hands with antibacterial scrub after caring for any quarantined animals.

Individuals without any other boas or pythons do not need to quarantine their new snake (unless they purchased more than one). But, for breeders or individuals with multiple specimens of boas or pythons, it is essential to quarantine new animals in individual enclosures, preferably in a separate room.

Quarantine new animals for as long as possible, ideally for at least a year; it may take a year or more for symptoms of IBD become apparent. Any animals that seem to be wasting away, exhibit neurological disorders (such as stargazing), experience chronic respiratory infections, or regurgitate their food on a regular basis require a veterinary exam and should be checked for IBD. At the very least, remove animals showing these signs from the area where healthy snakes are kept.

Obviously, breeders who have long-term established groups should be very cautious about introducing new animals into their collections. Several boa breeders have already been ruined by IBD.

Storeowners

At the very least, storeowners must try their best to keep larger boa constrictors bought from the public and breeders in individual enclosures. Dedicate a room for ridding new snakes of mites and to eliminate snake mites from the store display area. Only concerted efforts at all levels of the reptile market can help slow down the spread of IBD.

CHAPTER 3
SELECTING A BOA CONSTRICTOR

The initial selection of a boa constrictor determines the probability of your success at raising the animal to maturity, as well as the long term relationship you will have with it. The following guidelines will help you select a healthy, docile boa constrictor:

Captive-bred or Wild-caught?

When considering the purchase of a boa constrictor, the best choice is usually a captive-bred neonate from a reliable breeder. They are less likely to harbor diseases than imported boa constrictors.

Imported neonate to 2-foot boa constrictors are the next best selection. As a precaution, have the stools of any imported boa constrictors checked for internal parasites. In some imported groups of neonate boas that have been held

Smooth-Scaled Sand Boa

for long periods of time in the country of origin, respiratory disorders and gastroenteric disease become widespread and result in a high percentage of deaths. Typical symptoms involve bubbly mucus in the mouth and gaping (respiratory infections); and regurgitation, dehydration, loss of appetite, rapid weight loss, and deterioration (gastroenteritis).

Adult boa constrictors, particularly true red-tailed boas, vary considerably in their ability to acclimate to captivity. Imported adult boas harbor parasites and diseases that need to be treated before the boas can be successfully acclimated. Some adult boas, particularly adult red-tailed boas, may initially be reluctant to feed and may take several months to begin feeding on a regular basis.

Selection

Whether you are buying a captive-bred or an imported boa constrictor, pay careful attention during your selection protection. By watching for certain visual and physical clues, you can often determine whether a boa constrictor will be healthy and docile.

Use the following selection guidelines:

- Before handling an animal, select a snake that has a rounded body and does not demonstrate pronounced backbones or ribs. Check that the skin is relatively clear and free of superficial injuries. Avoid runts.
- Ask to handle the animal. Once in hand, a healthy boa constrictor should give a distinct impression of strength and good muscle tone. Avoid animals that appear limp or have poor muscle tone, both of which are reliable indicators of poor health. When moving, a boa constrictor will regularly flick its tongue. Unhealthy boas (such as those with respiratory infections) flick their tongues far less frequently. Unhealthy animals also flick their tongues with only slight protrusion of the tongue tips at a much slower rate than normal. If this symptom is present, other symptoms should confirm that the animal has health problems; these animals usually have poor muscle tone (weak snakes have weak tongue flicks) or bubbly mucus in their mouth.

Calabar Burrowing
Boa Cage.

- Next, perform the following steps to determine the snake's health status:

  Step 1: Hold the snake behind the head with one hand, and using the other hand, gently pull down the skin underneath the lower jaw to open the mouth of the animal. Look for the presence of bubbly mucus, which is a sign of respiratory infection. Another, though less-reliable, technique to determine this problem is to leave the mouth of the snake closed, and using your thumb, gently press against the throat area. If mucus emerges from the sides of the snake's mouth or nostrils, it probably has a respiratory infection. Avoid snakes with these symptoms.

  Step 2: Repeating the first procedure listed in Step 1 (opening the mouth), look for signs of mouthrot (stomatitis). The gums of an infected snake will be covered with caseous (cheesy-looking) matter. In some cases red, raw, and injured areas will be evident. Again, avoid animals with these symptoms.

  Step 3: Check the snake's eyes to make sure that they are clear. If the snake is in shed, both eyes should demonstrate equal levels of opacity (cloudiness).

  Step 4: Check the body for lumps, bumps, and depressed areas along the backbone. Check for collapsed areas along the sides of the body, which is a sign of broken ribs. Avoid snakes with any of these symptoms.

Step 5: Check the belly area to make sure that there are no signs of skin infection. Possibilities include raised ventral scales, stained or damaged scales, and other obvious signs of infection.

Step 6: Check the vent to make sure the anal scale lies flat against the body and is free of any caked or crusty matter. Make sure that the surrounding area is free of signs of smeared diarrhea. Avoid snakes with these symptoms.

Step 7: Look for mites, which are tiny, round, bead-like arthropods. When present, they can be seen moving on the body. They can also be seen imbedded between the rims of the eyes and the eyes themselves, giving a raised impression to the rims. On imported Colombian boas, mites sometimes cluster along, or inside, the rim of the snake's mouth. Two reliable indicators of mites are the presence of scattered white flecks (mite feces) on the snake's body and, following inspection of a snake, the presence of tiny mites crawling on your hands. If you have other snakes in your collection, avoid purchasing parasitized snakes. (See Diseases and Disorders.)

Docility

Some generalizations can be made about the temperament of boa constrictors. Generally, Colombian boa constrictors have the most docile temperament, while imported Mexican and Central American boas tend to be more nervous and aggressive. "Aggressive" behaviors in boa constrictors, such as striking and biting, are typically defensive reactions to perceived threats.

Many of the insular forms of boa constrictors, such as the Hogg Island, clouded, and St. Lucia boas, tend to be aggressive. All forms of boa constrictor are more docile and easily handled when raised from captive-bred neonates.

True red-tailed boas imported as adults from Guyana and Surinam also tend to be nervous and aggressive. In fact, for those who have never seen an angry boa, the hissing and striking of a large adult red-tailed boa will come as quite a surprise. Adult red-tailed boas that acclimate may initially be unpredictable, but with time and regular interaction, many settle down and allow themselves to be handled. Captive-raised true red-tailed boas, on the other hand, tend to have good dispositions and are easily handled as adults.

Number of Boas

Most households find that owning one or two boa constrictors is about all that they can handle. Keeping boa constrictors requires space, time, and tolerance for regular feedings of pre-killed, whole rodents. Captive breeding boas is difficult, unimportant to conservation, and rarely profitable. Boa constrictors are not endangered, and large scale captive-breeding will make you more of a farmer than a hobbyist; production and efficiency quickly become more important than the appreciation of individual animals. Furthermore, breeding boa constrictors, unless working with rare and expensive morphs, is a risky venture. The saturation of common reptiles and amphibians in the herpetocultural market has caused a drastic drop in the price of these species, and others factors, such as IBD, make it even more difficult and costly to be a successful boa breeder.

If you want a boa constrictor, enjoy your pet or your pair of animals, and care for them to the best of your abilities. If your pair breeds, the young may help offset the cost of keeping your animals and may make you a small profit. Though there may be some money to be made in breeding, only

Guyanan red-tailed boa constrictors are generally darker than other red tails. They tend to be more aggressive than other types of boas, but if captive raised and regularly handled, still become relatively tame.

This female albino Colombian common boa constrictor is the source of the Brian Sharp albino line.

purchase a boa if you feel that owning one enriches your life.

If your goal is the commercial breeding of boa constrictors, investigate the market carefully before making your decision. The herp market is fickle and subject to rapid changes. An initially expensive investment may drop considerably in value by the time you have babies for sale. Be wary of exceptional deals on nice adult animals. There are a number of unscrupulous individuals who will dump unhealthy and IBD-infected snakes. Proceed slowly and cautiously and read all the information you can on the subject. Some things can only be learned through experience, and there are no shortcuts to success.

Handling and Interaction

Regular interaction and gentle handling will make your boa more predictable and tolerant, and give it a better disposition. Establish handling routines with your pet boa; take it out two to three times a week for short handling sessions to make it more docile. As with many animals, there is variation in temperament among populations as well as individuals, and some animals will remain nervous and aggressive no matter how often they are handled. The best bet is to start with newborns and to use your judgment when selecting or handling adults.

Tame, regularly handled boas move in a calm but deter-

The original male albino boa constrictor that launched the Pete Kahl line of albino boa constrictors. Both Pete Kahl and Brian Sharp were responsible for propelling albino boas into the limelight.

mined manner, flicking their tongues at a regular rate and keeping the front of their body extended. Boas likely to bite usually provide ample warning for those able to interpret their behaviors. Nervous adult imported boas hiss, raise their heads above the ground, and form a coil in the front part of their body that usually precedes a strike. A frightened boa, when handled, also coils, sometimes hisses lightly, and performs slow tongue flicks, leaving its tongue extended for relatively prolonged periods of time. When handling animals that perform these potential pre-strike behaviors, use caution and avoid sudden movements. Instead, gently encourage the snake to move forward, or place the snake back in its enclosure until it settles down. During educational presentations, it is important to properly read a snake's behavior to prevent accidents. Small, excited children frequently make sudden movements that may alarm a snake. Under these circumstances, the snake may be uncertain whether it faces a potential enemy or an unthreatening human. Anybody using animals for educational purposes must pay close attention to their behaviors. Some snakes are perfect candidates for these types of demonstrations, while others may be too nervous to be reliable.

CHAPTER 4

HOUSING

There is a growing new school of thought about keeping reptiles in captivity. Instead of keeping them much like one keeps a laboratory animal, in small, relatively bare enclosures, those favoring the new approach focus on the captive animal's quality of life and the enclosure's display quality. Boa constrictors can be strikingly beautiful creatures, so why keep them in environments too unattractive to display in our homes? The recommendations in this book reflect the new approach to reptile environments. For those interested in keeping and breeding large numbers of boa constrictors, space- and labor-effective systems are preferable.

Enclosures

All snakes are masters of escape. If there is a way to get out of an enclosure, they will find it. So the first rule of snake-keeping is to buy or build an escape-proof enclosure with a locking mechanism designed specifically for snakes. Considering the time involved in building an enclosure and the costs of buying tools and materials, most people find that, unless they need a large number of enclosures, they are better off purchasing commercially-produced snake enclosures.

The most widely available snake cages in pet stores are all-glass tanks with sliding screen tops, and a pin to keep the screen locked. As long as one makes sure that the screen remains well secured to the frame, these relatively inexpensive and attractive enclosures work well with boa constrictors. Many boa keepers favor enclosures with sliding glass fronts, which are offered in specialty stores or by mail-order.

Neodesha Plastics, located in Neodesha, Kansas, is one of

the better known manufacturers of plastic-sided sliding glass-front enclosures that can customize certain features, such as ventilation openings. Vision Herpetoculture, in California, also manufactures plastic-sided sliding glass front enclosures with a thick tough plastic frame. Check the advertisements in herpetocultural magazines like *Reptiles* and *Reptiles USA* for other manufacturers. For top of the line, high-quality vivaria with black acrylic sides, an anodized aluminum frame, and sliding glass fronts, contact Vivarium Research Group, Inc., which manufactures beautiful vivaria that qualify as furniture. For larger boa constrictors, custom-made wood enclosures with glass fronts and sectioned-off rooms allow for the creation of attractive diorama type displays. Whatever your selection, make sure that your snake enclosure has a secure locking mechanism to prevent escape.

Size

A baby boa constrictor needs an enclosure at least 24 inches long (preferably 36 inches long), and 15 to 24 inches tall. Most adult boa constrictors require an enclosure at least 6 feet long, though small morphs, such as Hog Island boas and small adult male common and red-tailed boas, can be kept in 4-foot enclosures. If you want to include landscaping in an adult boa's enclosure, make sure the width of the cage is at least 24 inches and the height is at least 24 inches. Breeders keeping large numbers of adult boas usually purchase standard stackable 48- to 72-inch long enclosures from cage manufacturers.

Enclosure Design

If you want an uninteresting boa enclosure, keep your boa constrictor on newspaper with or without a shelter. It will feed, grow, and probably live a long time. However, it will not perform a wide range of behaviors, in part because it will be restricted by the sterile design of its environment. Likely, you will not spend a lot of time watching your boa in a bare setup.

If you are interested in an enjoyable display and in

observing a greater range of behaviors, enrich the vivarium with landscape structures, such as large tree branches placed diagonally and forming a resting site. Add cork hollows or above ground shelters. Then, your boa constrictor will do more of the things that boa constrictors do.

For example, in naturalistic vivaria, baby red-tailed boa constrictors often perch high in the enclosure, usually inside logs, but sometimes curled out in the open, making quite a nice display. All boa constrictors are nocturnal, sleeping during the day and becoming active at night. Although they may remain coiled in a shelter during daylight hours, they will be up roaming the branches at night. When they're in shed, boas tend to stay on the ground on moist soil, or inside a log with a moist bottom. I often find my boa con strictors basking under a light for a few hours in the early morning, but as the day warms up, they retire to a shelter.

Substrates

The most widely used substrate for keeping boas is newspaper. The advantages are obvious; newspaper is inexpensive, readily available, and easily replaced when soiled. The disadvantage is that it is unsightly. Visually more pleasing options are brown wrapping paper or newsprint. Herpeteculturists also use pine or aspen shavings as substrate for their boas. If you are a large scale breeder where efficiency is more important than looks, stick to newspaper.

Boa Enclosure; a combination of a pre-made and custom-built environment.

Recently, I have been using a high quality potting soil with no perlite (such as Supersoil), which is sold in stores like Home Depot and plant nurseries. If kept dry, the soil has a natural look, absorbs odor and liquid, and allows you to pick up fecal material in sections. Adding a layer of leaf litter gives an even more natural appearance. You can moisten the soil to increase humidity when a boa is in shed, or when the cage dries out; heated cages tend to dry out quickly. It can be replaced in sections as needed. For display purposes, as long as you provide shelters and other rest areas, soil mix has become my first choice as a substrate. However, potting soil is not a good substrate for gravid female boas to give birth on unless it is dampened and compressed.

When feeding boas kept on a soil substrate, offer pre-killed food on newspaper or with tongs and not on the soil surface. In boa constrictors' native habitat, the forest floor often contains clay and is covered with leaf litter.

Landscaping

The most widely used approach to keeping boas is housing them in the sterile-looking, bare enclosures used by commercial breeders. These types of enclosures do not include any features other than a ground level shelter, or a shelf that serves as both a perch and a shelter. Others keep boa constrictors in bare cages on newspaper. Though unappealing,

Another naturalistic setup. As a boa constirctor grows larger, the size of the perches and kinds of plants need to be replaced with sturdier varieties. Even very large boas could be kept with plants if you used trees in a room-sized enclosure.

this method works well for those with a large number of boas.

If you are interested in creating an attractive display and observing boa behaviors, provide boa constrictors with a varied landscaping as follows: a ground level shelter, diagonally resting branches with a horizontal fork for climbing and resting, and an above-ground shelf with an above-ground shelter.

Ground Level Shelters

Create an inverted U-type shelter with a height just slightly greater than the mid-body diameter of your snake for the ground level of your boa constrictor's enclosure. The shelters are easy to build; simply connect three or four wood boards with nails or screws. Wood hollows and large hollow cork logs provide a more natural alternative. You can also cover wood shelters with cork to give them a more natural look. Secure all heavy wood of any kind, whether branches or hollows, to the floor or walls of the enclosure to prevent accidental injury.

Climbing and Resting Branches

By introducing a sloping, easily climbed branch to the enclosure, you will be able to observe the arboreal activity of boa constrictors. To do this, collect or purchase a branch about the diameter of a boa's mid-body, and about one and a half times the length of the enclosure. It should have a nook or area about halfway down its length where two or three branches fork off. Place the branch in the cage and so that it slopes down across the enclosure, with its base resting on the floor against one wall, and the branches on top resting halfway up one or two other walls. Try to place the branch so that the forked section forms a horizontal resting area. Make sure the branch is securely anchored. In a very large enclosure, such as a sectioned-off room or closet, you can use more than one branch. However, do not clutter the enclosure with branches or use too many thin branches.

Above Ground Shelves

Some boa keepers try to add above ground shelters, such as anchored, hollow logs, to resting branches. An easier solution, if space allows, is to build an above ground shelf with its own shelter. Box–type shelters, inverted U-type shelves, or hollow cork logs all work well. Anchor the shelter with screws or L-shaped angle irons to prevent them from falling.

The Overhead Shelter Approach

For display purposes, shelters can create problems, because boas may stay in hiding most of the time. Positioning a branch or shelf under an overhang, such as the foliage of a live plant or a branch, creates a sheltered area that will keep a boa constrictor comfortable and visible.

The Risks of Naturalistic Displays

Designing larger and more complex vivaria for boa constrictors is not without risks. If not properly anchored, a landscape structure may fall and injure your boa. A boa may get scratched or stuck in certain places in the vivaria. Heat distribution in a large enclosure can be difficult to control, and as a result, may lead to increased risk of respiratory infection. Under certain circumstances, a boa may injure itself on the landscape structures or, in rare instances, die. Yet, for many who have gone the route of more naturalistic displays, the benefits of these setups generally outweigh the

A large Smooth-Scaled Sand Boa rests on a wooden shelf

Burrowing Calabar Boa cage environment.

risks, and are preferable to the sterile snake-in-a-box alternative. By carefully designing the captive environment and regularly observing your animals, you can predict and modify flaws in your vivarium and prevent these problems.

CHAPTER 5
HEATING AND LIGHTING

oa constrictors need to have a thermal gradient in their vivarium so that they can thermoregulate (control their body temperature). To create a thermal gradient, provide a moderately comfortable background temperature combined with a warmer hot spot, or basking area. By selecting between these two temperature zones, a boa constrictor will be able to maintain its desired body temperature.

Thermometers

The first step to providing a heat gradient is being able to measure temperature. This means you will need a thermometer. Several brands of inexpensive, compact stick-on

A young Colombian boa constrictor rests on an above-ground perch.

reptile thermometers are sold in the pet trade, and can easily be applied to the walls of a vivarium. Hardware and department stores sell inexpensive room thermometers that are also fairly effective.

Some of the most useful thermometers are digital thermometers; the best of these have an external probe and an indoor/outdoor switch. By placing the probe on the hot-spot and the thermometer at the cooler end, you get a continuous read-out of the background temperature and the temperature of the basking area. Digital thermometers are available in specialty electronic supply stores, such as Radio

A boa setup using an enclosure from Vivarium Research Group.

Shack, or by mail-order, from companies such as Edmund Scientific. Some even have an alarm feature that warns you when the temperature is outside of a set range.

Background Temperature

Keep the background air temperature in a boa enclosure between 80–85° F. At night, the temperature can drop to 78° F. It may be difficult to keep the air in a single snake enclosure at the right temperature without heating the entire room to the same temperature. Many people ignore the background temperature, and assume that the heat generated by the hot spot, in addition to providing localized warmth, will also dissipate and warm the air in the enclosure. This usually works during the warmer months of the year, but during the winter or in an air-conditioned room, a boa will spend most of its time trying to stay warm by remaining coiled on the hot spot of the enclosure. Persistent "heat hugging" is not normal behavior for boa constrictors.

In individual enclosures with screen tops, the easiest way to increase and maintain air temperature is to use a ceramic heat emitter (sold in reptile specialty stores), or to place an incandescent bulb in a reflector type fixture on the metal screen top. Take care to use the right wattage and to assure that the temperature in the vivarium is in the desired range. This can only be accomplished with a thermometer or a thermostat. Do not place these bulbs over the plastic edge of the vivarium or near flammable materials. Be attentive to all fire risks, and take every step necessary to safeguard them.

In wood or melamine enclosures with a solid top and sliding-glass front doors, you can attach the ceramic fixtures to ceilings as long as they are enclosed in a stiff wire basket to prevent the risk of thermal burns. If these bulbs are used in enclosures without screened openings, a thermostat is essential, and helps prevent the risk of overheating. Do not put these fixtures and bulbs near flammable materials, especially curtains.

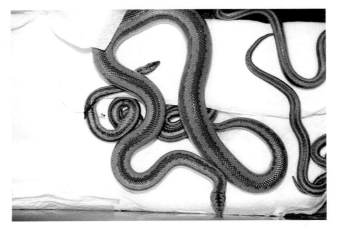

The inside of a walk-in environment of Desert Rosy Boas. Some walk-in environments provide shelves and heated platforms on the ground.

If you keep many reptiles in a small room, the various heat-generating units in or on tanks often raise the room temperature close to the desired range. If they do not, use a small space heater with a temperature regulating thermostat to keep the room temperature in the desired range. Follow its instructions carefully, and connect the heater to a back-up thermostat in case the heater's thermostat fails.

During the warm months or in warm areas, you may need to turn off heating units on warm days and use an air-conditioning unit to keep your boa's room at the right background temperature. In tightly sealed rooms or rooms receiving bright sunlight through closed windows, overheating is a common cause of death during summer heat waves. Temperature control is one of the most important care aspects for large scale breeders to consider. They should spare no expense and use back up thermostats, temperature warning systems, and fire alarms.

The Hot Spot

The warmest spot in a vivarium should measure 95° F, plus or minus 5° F when calibrated at the surface. There are three basic methods for creating a warm area in your boa vivarium.

Sub-tank Heating Units

Because most reptile enclosures sold in the pet trade are all glass with a screen top and recessed bottom, some of the most widely used heating units are thin heating pads placed under 25 to 30 percent of the tank. If placed under and covered by sheet metal, they can also be used in custom-made enclosures. If you plan to use heating pads in either setup, a working thermostat is essential. Do not use these heaters with plastic enclosures unless the manufacturer says it is safe to do so.

Heat Tape/Heater Strips

Flat, sheet-like heating units, popularly called heat tape, are sold in many reptile stores. Flexwatt, which needs wiring and assembly and should be connected to a rheostat, is available by the foot. Hagen sells a preassembled version of Flexwatt for the reptile trade, and T-Rex sells Cobra heat mats. Other similar units are available in the pet trade. Most keepers place these units under glass tanks, but they can be incorporated in the floor of custom-made enclosures. Connect them to a rheostat or a more sophisticated thermostat. If used without a way to monitor and control heat output and placed under tanks resting on solid surfaces, the heat may build up and crack the floor of the tank. An overly thick layer of substrate can act as an insulant and can also cause heat to build up beneath the tank, thereby causing the bottom to break.

To prevent heat buildup, leave a thin air space under glass tanks with sub-tank heaters. Simply raise the tank off the supporting surface and place thin sections of wood under the edges.

A Guyanan red-tailed boa constrictor. Striping and aberrant patterns can be caused by exposure to low temperatures during the later stages of embryonic development, so these characteristics are not often genetic in origin.

Sub-tank Adhesive Heat Pads

These are another variation of heat strips, but they have an adhesive surface for applying them to the bottom of a glass tank. ZooMed and other manufacturers offer such units. Use a rheostat or thermostat to control the heat output of these units. The greatest problem with adhesive heating pads is that they can get so hot that they cause the glass to expand and crack. To reduce the risk of this happening, avoid using a thick layer of substrate on the upper surface and avoid placing the tank on a solid surface, such as wood or carpeting. These surfaces seal the air space under the tank and cause heat build up.

Keep the enclosure on an aquarium stand, or place thin wood strips under the tank to allow some air flow to prevent heat buildup. Under rare circumstances, after cracking the bottom of the tank, the heat buildup will ignite inflammable substrates, such as pine shavings. Because of size limitations, these units are only suitable for small to medium boa constrictors.

Plumbing Heat Tape

In wood or melamine units, heat tape used to heat pipes in the winter can be placed in a groove running the length or width of an enclosure. Once the tape is in the groove, cover the top with metal sheeting to reduce the risk of fire and to help distribute the heat. Connect the heat tape to a rheostat or another kind of thermostat. Although this system is widely used by breeders, manufacturers do not recommend that plumbing heat tape be used in this manner, and take no responsibility for such use.

In-tank Heating Units

One of the simplest ways to create a hot spot is to use a heat-generating pad, which can be placed inside the enclosure. It should cover only 25 to 30 percent of the floor area. The following kinds are now available:

Plastic or Fiberglass Embedded Heating Units

These larger heating units are useful for providing heat to

larger boas. They are available either through specialized reptile stores or mail-order. It is very important that you follow the instructions for use. Most units cannot be covered with substrate because they run the risk of overheating. In such cases, fire is a risk. Generally, unless the manufacturer claims there is a built-in thermostat, regulate these units with some kind of thermostat or a rheostat. They are a good choice particularly when the use of sub-tank heating units is not possible, such as in room-size or plastic enclosures. A recent product manufactured by Bush Herpetological Supply comes in a size that makes it useful even with smaller boas.

Steel Embedded Nest Warmers
These units, sold for keeping poultry, work very well with reptiles and are available through reptile or bird supply companies.

Hot Rocks
These concrete embedded heaters are generally considered problematical for use with snakes, particularly if their surface temperatures are too high. The most common problems occur when a keeper leaves a snake in a cool room with no other heat source. Because snakes kept under cool background temperatures may spend extended periods hugging their hot rock, they may develop thermal burns on their belly and sides. To reduce the risk of this happening, use hot rocks only in conjunction with another heat source, such as an incandescent bulb. Because of their small size, hot rocks are suitable only for smaller boas, and need to be replaced with a larger heating system once a boa reaches more than three feet in length. Use a thermometer to measure surface temperatures. Some hot rocks are flawed, and can have burning hot areas that are easily detected by touch. Simply return these, indicate that they are defective, and request a replacement.

Incandescent and Infrared Bulbs
The third and final method for providing a basking area is to use incandescent bulbs or ceramic heat emitters. If placed

over an elevated shelf, these bulbs create a hot spot close to the heat source, and also provide background heat in the enclosure. The main problem with using incandescent light bulbs as a round-the-clock heat source is that they will remain on at night. Rather than facing this problem, use ceramic heat emitters as the primary, twenty-four hour heat source, and use fluorescent lighting connected to a timer as the daytime light source. To prevent burns, keep all bulbs used inside an enclosure in a protective wire basket. When used on screen-top enclosures, keep them in reflector-type fixtures, preferably with a ceramic base. Take great care to prevent the vivarium from overheating; this means selecting the right wattage bulb or heat emitter, using a thermometer to asses the temperature, and connecting these units to a thermostat.

Thermostats

Rheostats
Rheostats do not maintain a set temperature, but instead allow you to regulate the heat output of certain units, such as heating pads, strips, cables, and incandescent bulbs. In combination with a thermometer, they allow you to keep the temperature close to the desired range. Rheostats are commonly used to regulate the temperature of the hot spot.

On/Off Thermostats
These thermostats, the most common kind available, simply turn off a heating unit once the proper temperature has been achieved and turn it back on when the temperature drops too low. They are useful for controlling background/air temperatures.

Pulse Proportional Thermostats
Pulse proportional thermostats adjust the heating unit's heat output to the set temperature. They are the best choice for boa and reptile keepers. Biostat and Helix Controls are two of the better-known brands currently used in herpeto-culture.

Suriname red-tailed boa constrictors typically have a light coloration and red or brownish red tails. Many of the original red-tailed boas in captivity were imported from Suriname.

Lighting

Boa constrictors fare well with little light other than incidental light coming through windows or other light sources. Because boas tend to be active at night, many keepers argue that they do not require bright light. On the other hand, many boa owners have found that, in large enclosures, boa constrictors often bask on branches under a spotlight at different times of the day. Providing light also makes the experience of keeping boas more enjoyable. It enhances their display appeal, exposes the beauty of a well designed vivarium, and allows you to keep live plants in their enclosure. As long as the cage makes it possible, I recommend at least one incandescent bulb, both as a heat and light source, with boa constrictors. Place the light above a shelf or an angled branch, which will then serve as the basking site. In naturalistic vivaria, I also recommend full-spectrum fluorescent lighting, such and Vita Lites, for plants and general vivarium illumination.

Timers

The most trouble-free way to make sure lights get turned on or off is to keep them on a timer, which are readily available at hardware and department stores. For larger fluorescent fixtures, use three-pronged appliance timers.

Other Pets

Loose pets may knock over lighting fixtures, and this can result in fires. Do not allow dogs, free-roaming iguanas, cats, or any other pets in rooms with caged reptiles.

A young north Brazilian red-tailed boa. This broad saddled morph is representative of the descendants of animals originally collected around Belem. There are at least three different morphs of Brazilian red-tailed boas in captivity.

CHAPTER 6

FEEDING

Boa constrictors begin to feed soon after their first shed. As a rule, they feed readily at all sizes and rarely present feeding problems. The best and most readily available food for boa constrictors are commercially-bred rodents. Start feeding mice to baby boas, then switch to rats of an appropriate size as the snakes get larger, and eventually offer rabbits to large adults. Most boa constrictors readily feed on both live and pre-killed animals. Try to feed pre-killed rodents to your boas rather than live prey in order to prevent possible injury to the snake, and to minimize the suffering of the prey animal.

Prey Size Guidelines

The girth of prey items should not be greater than the girth, at mid-body, of your snake. Oversized prey items may be eaten, but are likely to be regurgitated at a later time.

Feed newborn boas recently weaned mice or pink rats. After a few feedings, offer small adult mice. If you offer prey of adequate size, feed your snake one prey item and then offer a second. If your boa constrictor is still hungry, it may feed on the second prey item. If not, it will usually leave it alone. By the time a boa constrictor reaches three feet in length, it will feed on small rats, and will accept bigger rats as it grows. However, continue to use the aforementioned guidelines for prey size (no larger than a snake's mid-body girth). By the time your boa reaches six to seven feet, switch it to large rats or small rabbits. Depending on their size, larger boas may eventually require large rabbits as their standard diet.

Live or Pre-killed?

Boa constrictors will accept pre-killed prey from the time

they are neonates. The advantage to feeding pre-killed prey is that it minimizes the possibility of bites and damage to a pet boa, and decreases the suffering of the prey animals. It also makes offering and removing prey an easier task. To humanely kill mice and rats, grab them by the tail and, with a swift motion, strike the back of their head against the edge of a table. With rabbits, the best method is to ask your supplier to kill them at the time of purchase. Experts recommended that keepers offer all prey animals, live or pre-killed, soon after removing them from their rearing cages.

It has been suggested that vitamin C and other nutrients that remain in the prey animal's digestive system after feeding may be beneficial to snakes. As with all predators, when a snake ingests its prey, it also ingests the gut contents of the prey. Thus, take care to feed prey animals a high-quality diet. Vitamin C, which can be provided by stomach contents, has been shown to play a role in reducing the probability of stomatitis, and in maintaining the integrity of the skin.

Other Foods

Some herpetoculturists occasionally feed their boa constrictors pre-killed whole chickens. Boa constrictors, like many other larger constrictors, like fowl of any type. Boas that otherwise refuse to feed often feed with great enthusiasm on chickens or other fowl. If your snake manages to escape, andyour family owns a pet bird, the bird is definitely in danger (as many people have discovered). Boas also readily feed on raw chicken parts obtained directly from the market (thighs, drumsticks, etc.).

However, use caution when feeding fowl in any form. A significant percentage of raw chicken parts test positive for salmonella and other disease-causing bacteria. If feeding live or pre-killed chickens, select your source carefully. In the best possible scenario, you should raise feeder chickens at home under relatively hygienic conditions. Many herpetoculturists pre-kill any fowl and freeze them for several weeks prior to feeding. The effectiveness of this procedure has not been clearly determined.

Use fowl only as a resort for fattening boas that are reluctant to feed (i.e., for imports or right before pre-breeding conditioning), and not as a standard diet. The feces of boa constrictors maintained on chickens for any length of time tend to be soft and smelly compared to feces of rodent-fed boas. This alone should be enough of a reason to use commercially-raised rodents as your boas' standard diet.

Feeding Regimen

A boa constrictor's growth is directly related to its feeding regimen. The growth rate is greatest during the first two to three years (at which point the snake reaches sexual maturity), and thereafter slows down considerably, though boa constrictors continue to grow for most of their lives.

Adjust your boa's feeding regimen to its growth rate and overall condition. Breeding females may also require a different feeding schedule to optimize their breeding condition. As a rule, you will have good breeding results with females that have good weight without being obese. After giving birth, females are often feed more frequently to make up for weight loss. Consider all these factors when determining feeding regimens.

"Power feeding" or "pushing" snakes by feeding them large amounts of food is not recommended with boa constrictors. Boas are not Burmese pythons. They don't grow as fast, don't appear to metabolize as fast, and overfeeding them can result in regurgitation, digestive problems, and obesity. This is particularly true of red-tailed boas and Argentine boas, which grow large over a period of years, in contrast to the two-year growth surge of snakes such as Burmese pythons.

Standard Regimens

From hatchling to 3 feet: Feed one to two mice of an appropriate size every seven days.

From 3 feet to 6 feet: Feed one to two rats of an appropriate size every seven to ten days, or every fourteen days for reduced growth rate.

From 6 feet and up: Feed one to two rabbits of an appropriate size every ten to fourteen days.

Proper husbandry and feeding will keep marvelous specimens, like this hypomelanistic morph of Argentine boa constrictor first produced by John Mack, healthy and vibrant.

Regurgitation in Red-Tailed Boas

Herpetoculturists sometimes report regurgitation problems with true red-tailed boas. Often associated with this syndrome are sticky, smelly stools. If in doubt, have a stool check performed by a veterinarian to determine the possibility of gastroenteritis. Usually, reducing the feeding schedule reduces the probability of regurgitation, but the primary cause of regurgitation syndrome in red-tailed boas appears to be insufficient enclosure temperatures. Maintaining red-tailed boas at temperatures of 87–90° F will often eliminate feeding and digestive problems encountered when rearing these animals. At these temperatures, true red-tailed boas grow at a greater rate and nearly match the growth of *B. c. imperator*.

Feeding Emaciated Boas

Imported boas sometimes arrive in an emaciated state, particularly smaller red-tailed boas. Many inexperienced herpetoculturists, upon the bad advice of even less experienced individuals, put these snakes on a heavy feeding regimen, either feeding them oversized prey or feeding them too frequently. This often results in regurgitation and death.

Before attempting to feed an emaciated snakes, first rehydrate it; dehydration can account for a significant portion of weight loss in imported animals. After the animals have had water for two to three days, offer a relatively small prey item,

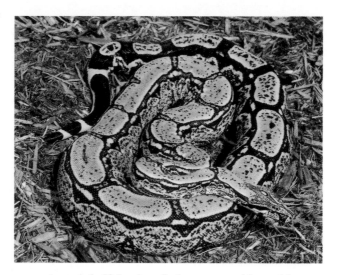

The "Arabesque" phase common boa constrictor is a distinctive morph with high-contrast patterns. It was first introduced by Steve Hammond of Exceptional Exotics.

approximately half the size of what one would consider normal prey for the snake. (The general rule of feeding prey with a girth no greater than the girth of the snake still applies.) Emaciated snakes have a much smaller body diameter than healthy ones. Feed one small prey item every five to seven days for three to four feedings, then feed two small prey items per feeding. Increase the prey size as the animal's body grows. During this process, keep the snake at relatively high temperatures (86–90° F) around the clock.

Proper Feeding Methods

Boa constrictors less than 6 feet in length can be fed without special precautions, other than being careful when placing food in or removing food from the cage. Once your boa reaches a size greater than six feet, it is critical to adopt safe feeding procedures to prevent the possibility of injury. In the case of boas, this means preventing the risk of being bitten.

The following are sound feeding procedures:

- Only house one snake per cage, and feed only one snake per cage at a time.
- Keep prey items within reach, and know where the snake is before opening door. If the snake is near the door, ready a snake stick to move it away. Open the door and move the snake away from the vicinity of the

door with the snake stick. Then grab the prey and toss it onto a suitable site in the cage, or introduce the prey item with a long pair of snake tongs. Under no circumstance should you hold a prey item in your hands (even by the tail or scruff of the neck) to offer to the snake. Don't be stupid.

- If the snake doesn't feed and you have to remove the prey, open the cage and, using a large snake stick, push the snake away from the vicinity of the prey and push the prey item toward the door. Remove the prey with a large set of tongs. Remove the prey with your hand only if the snake is at the other end of a large cage and well out of possible striking range. One safe method is to place a small board or a shield between the snake and yourself prior to removing any prey item.

Water

In the wild, boa constrictors are often found near water. In captivity, keep water regularly available in a large sturdy water bowl or, if you can afford the space, in a small pool.

Aside from providing drinking water, a water container also raises the air humidity in the snake's enclosure and provides an area for the snake to soak, which helps it shed. When using large pools, boa constrictors frequently defecate in the water. Be sure to use a container that can be regularly cleaned and disinfected in a 5 percent chlorine solution (unscented bleach from the supermarket). Fouled containers encourage the growth of microorganisms that can lead to disease. It is best to establish regular maintenance procedures and routines that account for this necessity. Commercial breeders often install small, easily drained utility sinks in their boa setups, which allows them to empty the water when it needs to be replaced and facilitates maintenance.

CHAPTER 7

MAINTENANCE

By adopting daily or weekly maintenance routines, you will be able to assure the long term health of your boa constrictor and prevent many of the problems encountered with this species. Always be attentive to changes in a boa's normal behavior. Regular observation of your animals and monitoring of the enclosure will help you spot potential problems early enough that serious consequences can be prevented.

Maintenance procedures:

Daily
* Perform a quick check of the enclosure, making sure that the lights and heater are functioning properly, and that the temperature is within the desired range.
* If the water is fouled or your boa has defecated in it, remove and clean the water container using an antibacterial dish detergent. Rinse it thoroughly and add fresh water. Remove and replace fouled substrate material.

This boa belongs to a new line of albino common boa constrictors thought to be tyrosinase positive. They were bred by David and Tracy Barker.

Remove shed skin when present.

- Without opening the enclosure or disturbing your boa constrictor, check that it is healthy and behaving normally.

Twice a Week
- Remove and clean the water container with an antibacterial dish detergent and a sponge. Rinse it thoroughly and return it to the enclosure with fresh water.

Weekly to Bimonthly
- Feed your boa constrictor an appropriate size, pre-killed rodent.
- Clean the glass front and sides of your boa enclosure.

Monthly
- Disinfect the water container by allowing it to soak for 20 minutes in a 5 percent bleach solution. Rinse it thoroughly and add clean water.
- Wash the inside walls of your boa enclosure with an antibacterial dish detergent. Wipe off the residue with fresh water. Some people also use a disinfectant to clean the inside of the enclosure.

A hypomelanistic common boa constrictor. The strain was originally developed by Jeff Gee of the Reptile Breeding Foundation.

Shedding

Like all snakes, boa constrictors shed their skin several times a year. Many first time owners inexperienced with this aspect of snake biology become concerned for their snake's health when they observe the initial changes associated with shedding. The first signs of shedding are a general darkening and dulling of the snake's skin, a process that lasts about a week. This is followed by clear signs that an animal is in shed: the eyes become an opaque, milky-white coloration, and the skin also acquires a dull, opaque, whitish cast. During this stage, old epithelial layers are pushed to the surface as the new epithelial layer of skin develops.

It is very important not to disturb or handle a snake during this "opaque" stage. There is a risk of damaging the new skin, and snakes cannot see well during this process, therefore making them more prone to defensive behaviors. Even normally tame snakes may strike out and bite when in shed. As a general rule, snakes do not usually feed during this stage, and keepers should not attempt to feed them. After three to four days, the opacity begins to clear. Three to four days after that, the boa begins the actual process of shedding. It will initially rub its snout and the edges of its mouth against rough surfaces to detach the skin edges. Once it frees the edges of its skin, the snake will slip out of its skin head first, the skin turning inside out as it propels itself forward. Following a shed, your boa constrictor will be at its most resplendent, with an unusually bright coloration and pattern.

Shedding Problems

Sometimes boa constrictors fail to shed properly, and some or all of the old skin may remain attached. The inability to shed properly can be a sign of environmental problems, such as low relative humidity or of ill health. (See Diseases and Disorders)

CHAPTER 8

BREEDING COLOMBIAN BOA CONSTRICTORS

By Jeff Ronne

The Colombian Boa is a highly variable, robust, and fascinating animal, and it readily reproduces in captivity if provided with the right conditions. The following information presents the model and methods I developed to breed my boas. However, my methods are not the only way to breed boas.

Before attempting breeding, there are certain conditions that must be met:

- You must have male and female boas of compatible size.
- They should be healthy and in prime condition (not thin or obese).
- Finally, you must cycle them properly and put them together. They will do the rest.

Sexual Maturity

In recent years, boa breeders have begun breeding female boas as young as eighteen months of age. The females give birth at about two years old and 5 to 6 feet in length. In order to achieve this large size in only eighteen months, the snakes require a very heavy feeding regimen. In my opinion, such a feeding schedule may lead to long term health problems. By controlling dietary intake, I raise males and females to 3 to 4 feet long in their first eighteen months. In fact, this size is large enough for most males to breed. In my experience, a 3-foot male will do a fine job breeding with a 6- to 9-

One of the outstanding Peruvian red-tailed boa constrictors produced by Jeff Ronne.

foot female. On the other hand, a courting 7- to 8-foot male can be very aggressive and may stress a 6-foot female, leading to an unsuccessful breeding.

Female boa constrictors as small as 4 feet long have reproduced in captivity. I have found muscle mass to be a good indicator of when a female boa is ready and able to breed. As they grow, boas tend to be long and lean until they reach about 5 feet long (three years) when they begin to thicken and develop more muscle. Although captive-raised boa constrictors initially fed enormous quantities of food grow considerably longer than this, it may require up to five years before they start filling out.

A mature, well-muscled 6-foot female may be the perfect breeding machine. A female this size, after parturition, easily gains back all of the weight necessary with regular feeding and will breed the following year. On the other hand, a large, 8- to 10-foot female boa constrictor may require an extra year or two to regain her pre-breeding weight. For this reason, a 6-foot female may produce more young over a period of years than a much larger female. Six-foot females also require less food and a smaller cage than larger specimens.

General Care and Husbandry
I keep my male boas in large plastic storage boxes. I breed my boas in one of three different types of enclosures. The

females' cages are made of melamine, which holds heat well. The cages are 2 feet wide by 4 feet long by 11 inches high; 2 feet wide by 4 feet long by 2 feet high, with a 4-foot-long, 22-inch-deep shelf; or 2 feet wide by 6 feet long by 20 inches high, with a 6-foot-long, 18-inch-deep shelf. All cages open at the front and have a hot spot at one end provided by Flexwatt heating strips, which are connected to a Helix Controls thermostat. The only illumination is the light that comes in through the windows. The ambient temperature is set at 82° F. The cages are on the ground floor to minimize vibration. When observing the snakes after dark, I use only a flashlight. Loud music, other pets, and smoking are not allowed in the snake room. Clean, fresh water is always available. I feed my boas every two to three weeks, and only handle the females when it is absolutely necessary.

Cycling and the Window of Opportunity

Female boa constrictors remain available for breeding for a relatively long period of time. Most breeders "cycle" their Colombian boa constrictors in much the same way that Burmese pythons are cycled. Typically, this involves a one month period of darkness (usually November or December), and exposure to lower temperatures (down to 70—75° F). After the cooling period, breeders raise the temperature and courtship and breeding commence. However, I believe this cooling period is unnecessary with Colombian

A Boa Constrictor eating a rat.

boas. It may, in fact, have negative effects, closing the "window of opportunity" for some females and unnecessarily disturbing for the breeding cycle of others. In my opinion, Colombian boas that reproduce after a cooling period do so in spite of the lower temperatures, not because of it. I maintain my boa constrictors at 82° F throughout the year, and the females always have a warmer area available in their enclosures.

At certain times of the year, boas constrictors refuse to eat or do so reluctantly. Such behavior is often the first sign that the breeding season has arrived. Usually, the snakes begin fasting in September. I stop feeding females boa constrictors at the end of September, and give them their last two meals two weeks apart, each consisting of prey one-third to one-quarter the size of what I normally feed them. I do not feed the females again until after ovulation, or subsequent to all breeding attempts. I feed the males their last meal in mid-August. Under normal conditions, the fasting period lasts between two to five months. The reduction of food intake and the shorter day length may be all that is necessary to cycle boa constrictors for breeding.

Pairing Your Boas

A breeding pair of boas need to be of a compatible size. Ideally, the male should not be larger than the female. They should be sexually mature, robust, and healthy animals. Generally, lean males make more ambitious breeders than fat ones. Smaller males tend to lack the energy to breed more with than one female, because the process takes six to twelve weeks of hard work per female. In my experience, a small sexually mature male is more likely to be an effective breeder than a larger more powerful male. I recommend having at least one male available per female.

Introduction and Courtship

When breeding boas, some breeders use multiple males, but I have found that this is unnecessary and less effective than using a single male. Although the presence of additional males enhances the competition to court, the victorious, or

more effective, male is often so intent on impressing the female that he is not relaxed enough to actually copulate. Another reason for using single males is to control the breeding outcome. Because selective breeding is of paramount importance in my breeding projects, it is critical for me to know which male fathered a particular litter.

First introduce the male to the female one week after the female's last meal. If ready to begin courtship, the male will usually demonstrate a lot of tongue flicking and move very slowly around the cage in an effort to follow and find the female, which (hopefully) is producing pheromones to attract a mate. The male should be left with the female for two to three days. If the male is not courting the female after this period, remove it, feed the female a small meal or two, and keep them separated for approximately three weeks. After three weeks, reintroduce the male following the same instructions as before.

This reintroduction procedure can be repeated three or four times in a single season and will enable you to take full advantage of the female's receptive period, which I call the "window of opportunity." Often, when the male is introduced to the female, he shows no interest in courtship. This may mean that one or both snakes are not yet ready to breed, or that they are not in prime health. Add another male to the enclosure to find out if the female is receptive.

When a male is interested in breeding, it will crawl on

top of the female, forming a zig zag pattern, and begin courtship by squeezing the female in five- to sixty-second intervals. The male will ride the female around everywhere it goes. The male may attempt cloacal alignment and will dig into or scrape the female's sides with its spurs. The female often acts irritated or annoyed by this scraping and tries to jerk away. Do not be alarmed by this behavior as it is part of the courtship necessary for successful breeding. Female boas develop egg follicles slowly over a period of weeks, maybe even months. The male's courtship may play a role in stimulating the continued development of these egg follicles. Courtship can be constant, taking place day and night, seven days a week. The occasional exception is when either of the two animals is opaque (pre-shed). Courtship lasts from three to eight weeks, after which time, the female may exhibit a posterior mid-body thickening. This is called the "pre-ovulation swell."

Pre-ovulation Swelling

Before the introduction of the male, the female often lies in an unusual position; it will stretch out straight in the vicinity of the ovaries, leaning slightly, showing small, discernible, tight curves while appearing very rigid. This is what I call the "pre-ovulation twist." I have noted this behavior in females prior to the male's introduction through just before ovulation. The maturing egg follicles often make the female appear gravid (which is normal), but the female is actually not gravid until after the fertilization of fully developed ova. This takes place after ovulation.

Females that have been courted by a male may begin to thicken. You may notice this swelling as early as two and one-half months before to ovulation, but it is normally apparent only two to three weeks prior to ovulation. The swelling is centered at a point approximately two-thirds down the length of the body. An obvious redistribution of weight will also be evident at this time. I believe that the misidentification of this swelling, or the assumption that the female is already gravid, may lead to the production of infertile ova (often called "slugs"). The incorrect assumption

Pre-ovulation swell in a female boa.

may cause the keeper to remove the male too early, resulting in low sperm levels or no sperm in the female to fertilize the ova. The length of the gestation period has also been greatly exaggerated because of this misunderstanding. Courtship, the pre-ovulation twist, and the pre-ovulation swell all take place before actual copulation.

Copulation

Copulation occurs after an extended period of courtship, and after the female has developed egg follicles. During copulation, a male inserts one of his hemipenes into the female's cloaca and deposits sperm. The actual mating may last for many hours. When copulating, the female's tail, just past the cloaca, will remain slightly lifted, with the male's tail lying alongside, rather than under, her tail. Male boas do not insert the entire hemipene, just the tip, leaving the cloacas slightly apart.

During copulation, the male will often curl its tail in the air, gently waving it, and occasionally making slight twitches. Copulation rarely occurs until the male has spent weeks courting and stimulating a female into developing egg follicles. Cloacal alignment is necessary for successful copulation, but the alignment itself does not mean copula tion is taking place. The male will copulate and rest repeatedly. It will ride the female for about a day or two and then rest for a day. It repeats this three to six times before eventually losing all interest in breeding (about one week before ovulation).

Ovulation

At the time the male ceases interest in breeding, the female typically turns darker. In the wild, this may be to enable the female to absorb more light to warm itself. Ovulation is the result of the fully developed ova moving into the oviducts for fertilization. The swelling associated with ovulation can be either massive or subtle, depending primarily on the size of the litter relative to the size of the female. The female will be stretched out with this huge swelling, while constricting and moving the ova through the oviducts. It will appear very uncomfortable during this process. The two ovaries can ovulate either together or separately, one to four weeks apart. I now regularly observe two ovulations in my boas, and believe it is the norm rather than the exception. The ovulation swelling is centered at the same location as the "pre-ovulation swell," slightly posterior from the half way point of the body. After the final ovulation, I raise the cage temperature to 84–85° F. Approximately five days later, the female goes into a shed cycle that I call the "post-ovulation shed."

Post-Ovulation Shed and Gestation

The shed cycle that follows ovulation is a little different from

Boa in Pre-ovulation swelling.

most shed cycles in that it takes sixteen to twenty-three days, which is longer than normal. After the post-ovulation shed, the female will remain darker than normal until the shed that follows the birth of her young. Resume feeding females after the post-ovulation shed, but do so sparingly. Most gravid boas continue to feed, but less aggressively than normal. I leave a pre-killed food item in the snake's cage overnight, and it is almost always eaten by morning. Offer a small to adult rat (depending on the size of the boa) three or four times, at two-week intervals, to help the female through the gestation period. I do not feed gravid females in the last four weeks of gestation to avoid causing the females to deliver premature offspring.

During the gestation period, gravid females typically move toward the warm end of the cage, and spend the night tightly coiled in an effort to minimize exposed surface areas and conserve heat. A small percentage of females have an intermediate shed approximately half way through the gestation period. Gravid females appear largest about two months into the gestation period. This time roughly corresponds with the period when the eggs of egg-laying boids swell and absorb water, probably to generate the needed albumen (birth fluid). A similar process occurs with live-bearing boids, and water availability during this period may be critical for the proper development of the embryos. Infertile ova do not have this fluid, so a female that is going to deliver slugs will never swell up very large. It will drop the infertile offspring approximately two weeks earlier than the normal projected due date. A female carrying a fertile litter gradually loses weight in the front half of its body and looks larger in the posterior half.

Generally speaking, the more emaciated the female looks as time progresses, the better. A female that is full of babies, with few or no slugs, looks worse than it would if it carried infertile ova. Within approximately two weeks of giving birth, the female appears dramatically thinner. This is the result of the developing embryos converting more of the yolk into muscle and tissue. The female also probably absorbs some excess moisture from the oviducts at this

Gravid female experiencing intermediate shedding. A small percentage of females experience this stage halfway through gestation period.

time. On occasion, the female will lie on its side or tilt sideways while gravid, especially during the last six weeks or so. Do not handle gravid females unless absolutely necessary.

Defecation and the deposition of urates occurs infrequently while the female is gravid. One or two days before parturition the female will defecate and deposit urates. This is pre-birth defecation is typically a waxy stool, and the fecal material at this time is moister on the exterior than normal, with a creamy appearance. When the female has a need to evacuate, it will position itself differently than while not gravid. It will stretch out, remaining extremely tense throughout its entire body, in an effort to push out the fecal material without prematurely depositing her young. This occurs like clockwork in every female just prior to parturition.

Parturition

Most boa breeders produce their babies in June and July. However, because I take advantage of the "window of opportunity" method, my boas deliver over a greater period of time. Although most of my boas' litters are born from March through June, I have produced Colombian boas in every month except September and November. Female boas, maintained as I have described, give birth, on average, 105 days after the post-ovulation shed, or 123 days after the final ovulation, give or take about five days.

A gravid female begins to get restless one to seven days before giving birth. She will cruise all over her cage, looking for the best place to deposit her young. You may observe the female moving constantly during this period, but don't be alarmed, as this is normal. The thick body mass often appears to move down slightly in the last week or so. Parturition usually occurs in the nighttime hours on a day when there is a drop in the barometric pressure. Rain or some precipitation usually accompanies this pressure drop. It is possible that, in the wild, rain may help mask or wash away the odor associated with the birth of the young. This "cleaning" may make the newborns less likely to become a meal for some other animal immediately after birth. Newborns, or probably the fluids associated with their birth, have a subtle but distinct odor, which I have noticed many times before actually finding the newly deposited young.

My females usually deliver their young under the ten to fifteen layers of newspaper I use as a substrate. When the female finds the best place to give birth, it will stretch out as much as possible along one wall of the cage, usually at the cooler end. It will tense its body and form a series of tight subtle 'S' curves, then begin contractions gradually and deliberately, and finally delivering her young. The neonates may come out in bunches or singly, inside or out of the membrane. I have found that boas born during the early part of the possible gestation period are more likely to still be inside the tough sack, usually with huge bellies full of yolk or a yolk sack still attached to them. Offspring born at the tail end of the possible gestation period are more likely to have absorbed all of their yolk, and emerge already out of the sack.

The birthing process can take as little as ten minutes, though it can take more than six hours. Generally, the higher the baby to slug ratio, the faster the whole process takes. Baby boas are born with a lot of albumen, as opposed to slugs, which are quite sticky and much more difficult to pass. An average 6-foot female should have about twenty-five neonates, and will have lost between 10—40 percent of its pre-breeding weight.

After parturition the female will be very tired. In spite of this, it often viciously defend its young, even if it had previously been quite docile. After delivering its young, the female sometimes takes a short, fifteen-minute rest before helping her offspring disperse. Different females seem to have different ways of accomplishing this. Some slide and crawl right through the mass of young, pushing them around with their sides, being very careful not to crush any of them. Others plow through the mass of babies with their heads, making quite a mess of themselves. Some females seem to be content to just watch over their offspring, tasting and smelling them with their tongues. Observing these behaviors, if you can do so without the female being aware of your presence, is one of the most rewarding and fascinating parts of being a herpetoculturist.

Infertile Ova, or Slugs

Herpetoculturists often refer to infertile ova as slugs, though

Burrowing Calabar Boa cage environment.

they sometimes use this term for fertile eggs that die in the earliest stages of development. Slugs are erroneously believed by some to be caused by insufficient cooling during the "cycling" process. In my opinion, slugs are usually caused by several mistakes made while maintaining and breeding boas. These include:

- Insufficient temperatures, which kill off sperm and newly fertilized ova;
- Exceedingly high temperatures, which destroy sperm and developing embryos;
- Insufficient water intake by the female, often caused by the lack of available fresh or clean water;
- Premature removal of the male, which normally continues copulating with the female until just before ovulation.

Post-Parturition Females

When I discover a litter of baby boas, I watch the female for a time to make sure she has completely ceased all contractions. I then remove the female from the enclosure and place her alone in a separate cage. She will eat with ferocity after having the young if she can not smell the residue of the birth process. The first meal is usually fed the day after parturition. Be careful, as the female will be uncharacteristically aggressive after having babies. This meal should be half the size of what the female is normally capable of eating at one time. One week later, I feed another meal the same size shortly after which the female will go into a shed cycle. After this shed, most females return to their pre-ovulation lighter color or close to it. Failure to do so or a reluctance to feed may be a sign that your female has retained part of the products of ovulation. If this is the case, a trip to your reptile vet is in order.

Newborn Boas

After removing the mother of the offspring from the cage, I soak the entire newspaper substrate with warm water and place a large water bowl, also full of warm water, in the enclosure. I then leave the babies alone. They usually all move to one spot in the cage away from the birth site, and in the process, scrape away any remaining birth fluid and debris adhered to them. Often one or two babies, or sometimes the entire litter, is slightly premature. Premature young have huge bellies full of yolk, and/or remain in the membrane. I keep those individuals moist by spraying them with warm water a couple of times a day, and otherwise leave them alone until they move off by themselves. Immediate removal of the babies may put unnecessary stress on the neonates, especially if they were born slightly premature.

Typically, baby boas are 16 to 18 inches long. However, I have seen viable young as small as 12 inches and as large as 23 inches. Normal full-term offspring shed when they are nine or ten days old. The first feeding is dependent on a couple of factors:
- Feed thin neonates that have absorbed all of their yolk right away, even before the first shed.
- Do not feed neonates that still have yolk in their bellies until the yolk is completely digested and they have gone through their first shed.

Offer a fuzzy mouse or pink rat at the first feeding, preferably fully thawed, pre-killed prey. If the first offering is not accepted, don't despair; simply repeat the process three or four days later, leaving the food item overnight (if you use thawed, pre-killed prey). You may need to use live prey items

Kenya Sand Boa giving birth.

for babies that do not eat after five or six attempts. Do not leave a live weaned rodent unattended with a baby snake, as the rodent may severely harm or even kill the young boa. As a general rule, feed all boas separately to avoid the accidental ingestion of another boa while feeding or, in rare cases, the death of both boas involved in a feeding incident.

Newborn boa constrictors have very delicate stomachs. I recommend that you feed small fuzzy mice or pink rats for the first ten feedings before moving on to larger food items. In general, pink and fuzzy rats seem to be much easier to digest than comparably sized mice. You must do everything possible to prevent regurgitation by baby boa constrictors.

Just the Facts

- Boas shed sixteen to twenty days after ovulation and give birth approximately 105 days after that shed, making the total gestation period approximately 123 days. This is also true for the following boas: Hog Island, Bolivian, Peruvian red-tail, Surinam red-tail, Guyana red-tail, and Argentine boa constrictors.

- In my captive litters, females are more common than males. To date, 52.5 percent of my babies have been female while 47.5 percent have been male.

CHAPTER 9

DISEASES AND DISORDERS

By Roger Klingenberg, DVM

Any pet, reptile or mammal, is likely to have some particular health concerns, and boas are no exception. While boas enjoy relatively good health, they are susceptible to some ailments of which the reader needs to be aware. As is true for all types of reptiles, poor husbandry practices and ignorance of pertinent natural history are responsible for most problems. With the exception of IBD, most boa ailments are very similar to those seen in other snakes, although they may be precipitated by different circumstances.

Inclusion Body Disease

Inclusion Body Disease, a fatal viral disease, is without a doubt the most significant disease in boid snakes. It is much more prevalent than is currently realized, and the emotional and economic damage wrought by this disease defies estimates. If the reader learns nothing else about boa health, hopefully it will be an awareness of IBD. Because IBD is often the underlying factor in other diseases, I decided to present the little that is known about IBD as the first topic in this chapter.

IBD is not a new disease, nor did it sneak up on herpetologists from obscurity. It has been recognized as a disease syndrome for more than twenty years, but isolation of etiologic agents was accomplished only in the last few years. The presumed etiologic agent is a retrovirus (in same category of viruses as HIV), and the boa constrictor appears to be the

This boa was contorted and exhibited a dulled mental state. It maintained the ability to right itself, but couldn't control its movement. All of these symptoms indicate the chronic stage of IBD.

normal host. Retroviruses do not survive well outside the body so transmission appears to be from direct contact with carriers, or their body fluids. It is possible that snakes maintained in a cage together, while at risk, may not immediately acquire the virus. Over time, the likelihood of exposure to body fluids through breeding, bites, urinary and fecal contamination, and nasal or salivary secretions greatly increases the risk. Mites and ticks, by virtue of feeding on body fluids, may also serve as vectors. Many reptile authorities are convinced that mites are responsible for the spread of this disease through entire colonies of otherwise well-maintained snakes.

One of the more frightening aspects of this disease is that it can lie dormant in boas for months or years. In research being conducted at Berkeley, Dr. Dale DeNardo reports that confirmed IBD positive boas have remained perfectly healthy for more than fourteen months (and counting). These IBD carriers appear to be perfectly healthy, without signs of illness. The ability to be a long-term carrier is perhaps the strongest evidence that boas are the natural host of the virus.

What causes the virus to become active? Is it related to the length of infection, or does a breakdown of the immune system allow it to progress? Researchers don't yet know the answers to these questions, but most assume that stress factors likely predispose boas to active cases.

This boa, which exhibited severe contortions, an in ability to right itself, and a dulled mental state, was an obvious candidate for IBD. This boa, however, was found to have bacterial meningitis, not IBD.

At this point, IBD appears to affect only boid snakes. Pythons appear to be atypical or aberrant hosts, as the disease is much more acute than in boas and progresses rapidly. Research has not proven that pythons are long term carriers, but Dr. Elliott Jacobson believes he has seen a change in the behavior of the virus in Burmese pythons over the previous two decades. A typical python with IBD presents dramatic neurological signs, ranging from mild stupor to seizures. Supportive care may help to stabilize the patient, but its death is inevitable. Dr. Jacobson has pointed out that Burmese pythons afflicted with IBD twenty years ago also exhibited prominent neurological signs. He now sees Burmese pythons that present chronic respiratory diseases as the initial sign of IBD. Does this mean that Burmese pythons are evolving to mount an immunological response to the virus? Is the virus changing? As yet, these answers also remain elusive.

By examining a couple of typical cases, the insidious nature of this disease will become apparent.

Case 1

A reptile owner decides she would like to have a new boa constrictor as a cagemate for her current boa constrictor, and locates one through the want ads of a local paper. She is not interested in breeding the pair, and is not even sure of the gender of her boa. She agrees to buy the snake, and she immediately places the new snake in with her pet boa, confident that having a cagemate will improve the quality of life for both snakes.

Several weeks later, the reptile owner is frustrated to find that her snakes are covered with small, black bugs that her roommate, the proud owner of an eight year-old ball python, informs her are snake mites. The women call their local reptile veterinarian, who requests an examination before prescribing a mite product, so they elect to make a quick visit to their local pet store instead. After obtaining some over-the-counter mite products, they wage war on the mites.

During the intensive cage cleaning, they notice that the new boa is exhibiting some open-mouth breathing and has a thick, copious saliva. They return to the pet store with the sick boa in hand. The pet store employees advise them that the snake has mouth rot in addition to the obvious respiratory infection, and advises them to see their veterinarian. Because money is short, they decide not to go to the veterinarian, and instead take a sulfa-based medication home, and increase the cage temperature.

While the snake initially improves, it will not eat, and shows up dead in its cage a few weeks later. Devastated, the reptile owner buried the dead snake in her yard. Because the other boa is still in good shape and is free of mites, she buys a new boa cagemate for it from her pet store. All is well for a few weeks, when the roommate's ball python is found in its cage, upside down. The ball python is unresponsive, and unable to flick its tongue or right itself. A friend suggests that the snake might have a brain tumor and volunteers to dispose of the snake for them. The roommates are so distressed that they decided to trade their two remaining boas to their pet store for some guinea pigs, cages, and supplies. The boas are eventually sold to two other separate owners. One of these owners brings the boas to his veterinarian because it has chronic infections, and the veterinarian diagnoses it with IBD.

Case 2

Another reptile owner purchases a two year old male boa constrictor from a close friend to use as a breeder for two female boas he has owned for three years. Our reptile breeder is well informed, so he quarantines the new snake in a separate room for three months. He even has a "well pet" visit with his reptile veterinarian, who determines that the snake appears healthy, and is free of internal parasites.

Breeding season is approaching, so the owner puts the boas through a short cooling period to stimulate spermatogenesis and ovulation. During the cooling period, the new male develops raspy, open-mouthed breathing, and the owner promptly takes it to his veterinarian. The veterinarian diagnoses it with a mild respiratory infection, and prescribes treatment with systemic antibiotics and an increase in cage temperatures. The male responds well and tolerates another brief cooling period prior to being placed with the females for breeding.

Breeding is accomplished without incident, and our reptile breeder is rewarded with twenty-one viable offspring, which he sells to friends, local pet stores, and even sends five to a friend out-of-state. Our breeder is concerned that one of the females doesn't eat as voraciously as it had after previous litters, and that it has some minor mouth lesions, which his veterinarian diagnosed as infectious stomatitis. The mouth rot is successfully treated by topical cleaning of the infected tissues, and by administering a systemic antibiotic. The female regains weight and our breeder enjoys another rewarding breeding season.

What do these cases have in common? For one thing, they are both actual cases that I have encountered, though my place in both took place later than the events described. Secondly, they both represent IBD infections.

Look at the first boa owner's dilemma (Case 1). Which boa brought the virus into the group? It could have been the newest boa that the owner bought as a cagemate, or just as easily, it could have been the original boa. The stress of the boas being placed together, along with sub-optimal cage conditions, was likely sufficient to cause the newest boa's immune system to become impaired, and allow secondary illnesses the opportunity to invade. The fact that IBD was involved with the breeder (Case 2) was not evident until one of the offspring died, and was then euthanized, necropsied, and diagnosed with IBD. Subsequent testing of both of the breeder's male and female boas were positive for the virus. As the females had been in his collection for more than three years, it was more likely that the new male had brought the virus into the group. However, this is impossible to prove, because one of the females may have been a long-term carrier.

Hopefully these examples illustrate how easily the disease can spread. In the first example, the boas returned to the pet store resulted in one confirmed IBD case and one boa that was exposed to and likely infected with IBD, but was impossible to locate. In the second example, some of the infected offspring were located, but the majority were not found. This is exactly the same scenario that has happened in the last couple of decades. There is absolutely no doubt that this disease is not only widespread, but much more prevalent than keepers, herpetologists, and veterinarians realize.

What can boa owners do to protect themselves from acquiring a snake with IBD? (See the sidebar following for more information.) We need to first look at how IBD is diagnosed. At this time there are no simple diagnostic kits or tests available. Veterinarians confirm the presence of the disease by observing intracytoplasmic inclusion bodies in infected tissues. The significance of these inclusion bodies is not known, only that they occur in any epithelial origin tissues, and in the neurons of the central nervous system.

In my practice, I first take a sample of the suspect boa's blood. I perform a complete blood cell count (CBC) to look for elevated white blood cell (WBC) levels, which Juergen Schumacher's classic study found to be seen in the early stages of IBD. Schumacher's group also found inclusion bodies in a number of circulating white blood cells, but not in red blood cells. I have rarely seen elevated white blood cell counts in affected boas, but have noted that a high percentage of active cases have inclusion bodies in circulating red

Tissue biopsies, especially of the liver, kidney, esophageal tonsils, and gastric mucosa, are the most reliable means of diagnosing IBD. This section of the liver has several eosinophilic (red) staining inclusion bodies.

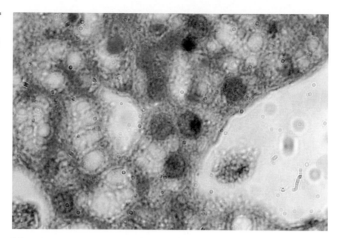

blood cells. Dr. Terry Campbell, at Colorado State University, also verified seeing inclusion bodies in red blood cells.

Protecting Your Collection from IBD

- Buy your boas and pythons from experienced, reputable dealers. This does not guarantee perfect health, but established dealers need repeat business and a good reputation. Dealers almost always know the history of their snakes.

- Quarantine all new pythons for three months, and all new boas for at least six months. This may not keep your collection free of infected boids, but it will give you time to eliminate mites and further quarantine unhealthy animals. In ideal situations, you should not mix boas with other boas for more than a year.

- Do not add or give out boas and pythons for breeding unless you adhere to strict quarantine procedures.

- Do not care for other snakes (belonging to other people) in the same house or establishment that you keep your snakes.

- Use fastidious hygiene practices when caring for your collection. Wash your hands and clean any pertinent materials (gloves, tongs, etc.) between handling snakes. Keep the cages clean, and do not rotate cage furniture or uneaten prey between cages.

- Never add an unhealthy snake to your collection, even those that seem too good to pass up. Do not adopt free or inexpensive boas whose history is unknown. Adopting a free, IBD-infected snake may be the most costly mistake you ever make.

- Consider all unhealthy boas and pythons to be possible IBD carriers, especially those exhibiting signs of CNS problems. Consult a veterinarian for further assistance.

Do these differences mean that the host or the virus are changing? Are we seeing new strains of the original virus? Again, there are more questions without answers. If a veterinarian does not find inclusion bodies in the red blood cells, then the next step is to perform tissue biopsies. In my experience, a liver biopsy is the easiest and least invasive procedure, and data suggests that 70 percent of positive animals will be identified with this technique. Schumacher's study indicated that inclusion bodies were found in 100 percent of pancreatic biopsies, and in 70 percent of liver and kidney biopsies. The pancreas is extremely difficult to locate and is not a forgiving organ to disrupt. The liver is a large organ, has a predictable location, is easily accessed, and heals well following biopsy.

Unfortunately, if inclusion bodies are not located in the blood smears or on a liver biopsy, the animal still cannot be considered free of the disease. Quarantine suspect cases for up to another year or obtain additional tissue biopsies obtained. Dr. Jacobson routinely obtains biopsies from the esophageal tonsils, the gastric mucosa, and the liver to increase the odds of finding inclusion bodies if they are present.

A less conventional method to detect the presence of the virus could include housing a more susceptible python specimen (i.e., a ball python) with a suspect boid. Theoretically, the more susceptible python would succumb to the disease, if it is present, within three months.

The need for a blood-based diagnostic test is obvious. The technology necessary for the development of such a test has existed for many years, and one industry expert said a test could be developed and available within six months, if the economic viability of such a test were warranted. Research is ongoing at Florida State University's Veterinary School under the direction of Dr. Jacobson, but at the cur-

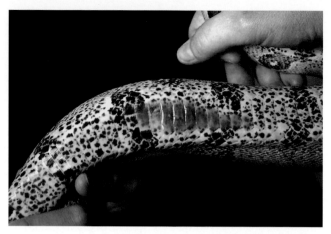

The dark, reddish, fluid-filled vesicles on this boa's abdomen are an early sign of necrotic dermatitis (scale rot). The appearance of these vesicles, also called blister disease, is an early stage of a skin-based infection. If not properly and aggressively treated, the problem will destroy the surface scales and cause severe ulceration.

rent rate, could take years to develop and produce a commercially available product. Once developed, the product could be used to test snakes at the point of import to determine carriers, and it could diagnose pet snakes through a simple blood test.

I predict that the day will come when the purchase of a boa includes a microchip implant for identification, and a certification of IBD status linked to that identification. However, the day of IBD-free boas will not occur without the input and assistance of herpetoculturists.

First, herpetoculturists need to convince the medical diagnostic community that a blood test for IBD is necessary (in other words, that people will pay to have their snakes tested). Reptile owners need to tell their veterinarians that they want this diagnostic technology. The veterinarians, in turn, will pass this information on to the companies that produce these tests. Secondly, the reptile-keeping community must provide funding for the initial phases of this research (see following sidebar for information on contributing to IBD Research). Thirdly, the reptile community must ensure that its own members do not to sell or trade known infected animals. Knowingly trading an IBD-positive animal to an unsuspecting party is morally reprehensible.

Contributing to IBD Research

Herpetologists, hobbyists, and breeders have contributed more than $25,000 to the University of Florida's IBD research team. Despite the generosity, this sum is woefully short of the amount needed to support ongoing work. Anyone interested in the welfare of boas and pythons should consider supporting this project. To make a donation, contact Dr. Elliot Jacobson, College of Veterinary Medicine, Dept. of Small Animal Clinical Sciences, University of Florida, P.O. Box 100126, Gainesville, FL 32610-0126.

There are no known treatments for this viral disease. Intense supportive care aimed at eliminating secondary infections, and providing for nutritional and hydration concerns may keep the snake alive, but it will not eliminate the infection. Due to the contagiousness of this virus and the inability to eliminate it, euthanasia is a valid consideration.

Respiratory Disease

Respiratory disease in boids is almost always due to suboptimal husbandry practices, especially the lack of a useable heat gradient. Current veterinary knowledge places a great deal of emphasis on the provision of heat as a means to support physiological functions and behavior in reptiles. A thermal gradient that reaches the upper Preferred Optimal Temperature Zones (POTZ) improves digestion and activ-

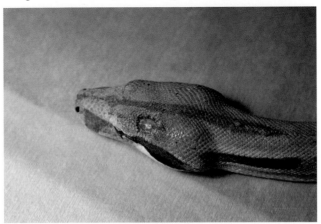

This boa was severely bitten at several locations, including the eyelid, by a live rat. To prevent this problem, feed fresh-killed or thawed rodents to your snake.

ity, and is the easiest way to support the immune system. Immune system support is important to prevent medical problems, and to augment treatment when they do arise. Numerous studies have demonstrated that reptiles with access to such thermal gradients produce a better coordinated immune response, including better antibody production, better cellular mobilization, and improved suppression of pathogens. Reptiles can create a "behavioral fever" by selecting warmer areas when they are ill.

Early respiratory disease is characterized by noisy or raspy breathing, and a tendency toward open-mouthed breathing. Exposure to a thermal gradient often stimulates the immune system adequately to resolve the infection. Continued stress factors, such as inadequate heat, will cause a low grade respiratory infection to worsen. As the infection progresses, the respiratory system increases mucoid secretions in an attempt to dilute and expel bacterial pathogens. These emissions first appear as foamy, mucoid secretions from the corners of the mouth. If you looked inside the animal's mouth, you would see these secretions coming from the glottis, and collecting in the back of the throat. The snake's pen-mouth breathing will become more evident, and it may start lying against the sides of the cage in an effort to drain secretions out of the narrow trachea.

Snakes do not have a diaphragm, and to their detriment, cannot cough. Coughing is a very useful mechanism for

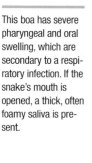

This boa has severe pharyngeal and oral swelling, which are secondary to a respiratory infection. If the snake's mouth is opened, a thick, often foamy saliva is present.

clearing airways of tenacious secretions. Any "coughing," popping, clicking, or wheezing noises made by snakes are due to air forced through fluids and debris trapped in the narrow trachea and congested lungs. Chronic partial blockage of the glottis and trachea can result in a distended pharyngeal region or throat, as the snake will distend this area in an attempt to open the airways.

Once the snake reaches this stage, you must implement much more aggressive intervention to prevent it from suffocating, or literally drowning in its own fluids. Seek experienced veterinary care. A veterinarian will hospitalize an afflicted snake at temperatures near the top of their POTZ range to stimulate its immune system, and to help keep the respiratory secretions viscous. The veterinarian will prescribe or administer systemic antibiotics, and obtain and process a culture.

Place branches or containers in the snake's cage so that the snake can rest in an upright position to aid breathing. If breathing is impaired, nebulization with bronchodilators, expectorants, and/or drying agents is utilized. In the event that a boa owner cannot get his or her snake to a veterinarian immediately, increase the cage temperature, and use a vaporizer with saline (an excellent expectorant) to help the snake survive.

This boa's nose and upper lip are swollen and distorted by a friable and crusty material subsequently diagnosed as a fungal infection.

Gastrointestinal Problems and Regurgitation

One of the most common complaints of new boa owners, especially those working with newborns or juvenile boas, involves regurgitation. With juvenile snakes, both overfeeding and inadequate heat are often possible causes. Although young boas will readily eat every few days, it is more prudent to feed less often. If a boa stuffs its digestive tract with newly acquired foods to complement foods that are still being processed, the gastrointestinal (GI) tract can become irritated and expel its contents. It is better to feed a sensitive boa once every seven to ten days and allow for digestion to progress before feeding again.

Certain boas, especially Surinam boas, need to have a warm basking area after feeding or regurgitation will occur secondary to maldigestion. For young snakes that are regurgitating, initially stop feeding them, then try feeding smaller meals less often, as well as providing a warm spot to aid digestion.

Adult boas may also regurgitate after being fed excessively and being kept in insufficient temperatures. However, it has been my experience that most adult boas regurgitate after protozoal flare-ups. Most reptiles have low levels of

Regurgitation seems to be a rare sign of IBD. However, it is not unusual to find significant pathological lesions in the GI system of necropsied boas affected with IBD. The severe inflammation and swelling of the stomach tissue from this IBD boa illustrates how regurgitation could be induced.

protozoal organisms in their digestive tracts that do not cause ill effects. However, if GI dysfunction occurs for whatever reason, these same protozoans can overpopulate the

Rostral abrasions, like those shown here, are usually due to a poorly constructed or uncomfortable cage. Minor abrasions may require nothing more than antibiotic ointment, but deeper wounds can destroy the scales and lead to permanent disfuration.

tract and cause pathology. To treat this problem, withhold food for several days, administer oral metronidazole (Flagyl) at 50 milligrams per kilogram of the snake's body weight (mg/kg) daily for three to five days, and then reinitiate feeding with small, gradual meals.

While Juergen Schumacher's group reported that the number one clinical manifestation of IBD in boas was regurgitation, DeNardo and I have not found this to be a consistent presentation. Other potential causes of regurgitation include bacterial gastroenteritis, GI foreign bodies, tumors, cryptosporidiosis, and systemic disease. Persistent regurgitation problems that don't respond to treatment should be investigated by a qualified reptile veterinarian.

Constipation

Constipated boas are usually diagnosed both from their history and from physical signs. Although reptile owners are encouraged to keep accurate records, many do not record bowel movements. However, reptile owners should be aware of any snake that has not had recent bowel movements, is bloated, or has stopped feeding. It is interesting to note that even some severely constipated boas will continue to eat, so appetite may not be a good indicator of constipation.

By palpating the snake's lower abdomen above the cloacal vent, you can feel retained fecal and uric acid accumulations. Palpate the abdomen by gently pressing up on the

Retained eye caps are generally due to a lack of relative humidity. Do not force them off. Note that the rostral scales are also constricted due to the chronic irritation of dry skin.

area, or by letting the snake crawl over the fingers.

Constipation in boas appears to be primarily due to two factors: dehydration and a lack of exercise. Dehydration can occur in cages that are well heated, but dry due to the high evaporative rate. Remember that boas are tropical snakes, and they require moderate to high humidity. Some herpetologists suggest that the feeding of frozen/thawed rodents is also a cause of dehydration. They postulate that the freezing process reduces the rodents natural body fluids; the longer the freezing, the greater the loss of fluids.

It is very important to hydrate constipated boas. The easiest method is to allow the snake to soak in shallow, tepid water for an hour or two each day. Even if a boa doesn't drink, it often takes on water rectally, due to the relaxation of the anal sphincter when soaking. Refractory cases are best treated by a veterinarian, who will often administer fluids and enemas. Occasionally, the snakes require light sedation, and the veterinarian will manually remove the fecal material by gently pushing it toward the cloaca from the outside. Prevent dehydration by providing adequately sized water dishes, lightly misting the cage daily, or by injecting fluids into thawed feeder rodents.

Adult boas, especially those that are overfed, tend to become true couch potatoes.

If large boas are confined to small containers, it also limits their activity level. This inactivity also contributes to the onset of constipation. It is important to remove your boas from small enclosures and allow them some exercise at least twice a week.

Parasitism

Many boas tend to lack intestinal parasites. Whereas 99 percent of ball pythons collected in the wild have internal parasites, only 25 percent of wild collected boas have internal parasites. If maintained properly, captive-born boas are virtually parasite free. Despite this relative lack of parasites, I still encourage you to take your boa in for a fecal examination. Your snake could be the one out of four to be affected.

Nematode parasites are easily treated with oral fenbendazole (Panacur), at 50 mg/kg once a week for three to four weeks. Treat cestodes with praziquantel (Droncit), at 5 mg/kg either orally or injected, and then repeat the treatment two weeks later. Treat protozoal infections with metronidazole (Flagyl), at 50 mg/kg orally, daily for three to five days.

External parasites include both snake mites and ticks. Remove ticks with tweezers or forceps by grasping the body and steadily pulling them out. Apply antibiotic ointment to the site of tick removal, and add a systemic antibiotic if a non-healing wound results. Inspect the snake for ticks two to three times weekly until you do not find any more.

Treat mites with an ivermectin spray, made by adding 5

This Argentine boa has a distorted upper lip due to an infected tooth. With the mouth opened, it is easy to see the fluid-filled swelling.

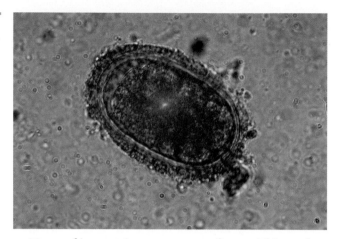

An ascarid ova (roundworm) characteristic of those found in boas. Pictured at one-hundred times magnification.

to 10 mg of ivermectin to one quart of water. This product is thought to remain stable for approximately thirty days, after which time you can mix a new batch. Apply the spray lightly, but thoroughly, to the entire snake, including its face, labial pits, throat, and vent. Remove your snake's water dish, and spray the cage (inside and out) thoroughly after cleaning. Return the snake and water dish to the cage after it has dried. Repeat this procedure every four or five days for three weeks.

Although I have had excellent results with this very dilute spray, one death was reported in a juvenile boa after its use. The young boa would have had to ingest nearly four to five milliliters of the spray to even reach recognized oral levels, sometimes used to clear internal parasites. Subsequent pathology work on the baby boa concluded that it was possible that an idiosyncratic reaction to the ivermectin may have occurred. In other words, the boa was extremely sensitive to the drug. Every product carries some risks and the reader should be so advised.

Salmonellosis

Owners who feed chicks or chickens to their boas expose their reptile to potential salmonella infections. *Salmonella sp.* are currently being isolated from a number of common reptile species. It is now well recognized that many reptile species can harbor salmonella bacteria, and serve as asymp-

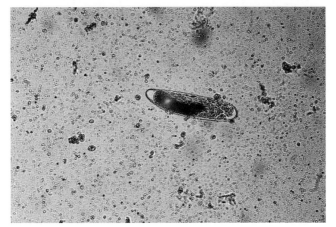

An oxyurid ova (pinworm) found in an Argentine boa. Pictured at one-hundred times magnification.

tomatic carriers. Boas have been mentioned less commonly as salmonella carriers, but I have isolated salmonella from osteomyelitis lesions, and in IBD respiratory infections. The point is that the vast majority of salmonella cases in humans are caused by consuming raw or poorly cooked chicken products. Why risk feeding raw poultry products to your boa when most readily accept rodents?

This young boa has bulging eyes, caused by a mite invasion of the periorbital space.

Anatomical Region	Symptoms	Common Cause	Treatment
Eyes	Opaque, wrinkled film on eye	Retained eye cap	Increase humidity with a light misting. Apply artificial tear ointment to the eyes twice daily until the cap loosens. Do not forcefully remove it.
	Enlarged and bulging eye	Eye infection; postorbital abscess; glaucoma; eye trauma	Seek veterinary assistance. This problem may require both topical and systemic medication.
	Puffy eyes; elevated rim of eye	Mite infestation of postorbital space	Apply artificial tear ointment daily to suffocate mites. Use a small sexing probe to physically remove mites. Experts also recommend general mite treatment.
Nostrils	Occluded nostrils; Open-mouth breathing	Retained shed; dried secretions from respiratory infections	For retained shed skin, apply artificial tear ointment twice daily until it loosens. If necessary, use a blunt probe to remove it once it loosens. Watch for signs of respiratory disease.
	Raw, swollen, or abraded nose	Rostral Abrasion	Evaluate the cage size and design. Remove all sharp edges. Treat mild abrasions with Neosporin or Polysporin.
Mouth	Mild distortion; hemorrhage spots; viscous secretions; cheese-like pus; excess salivation	Infectious stomatitis; infected teeth	Increase the temperature of the enclosure. Loose teeth and damaged tissues require surgical removal, followed by a cleansing with dilute nolvasan, dilute betadine, or peroxide. If the problem persists, see a veterinarian.

Anatomical Region	Symptoms	Common Cause	Treatment
Throat	Distended or inflated throat	Respiratory infection	Increase the temperature of the enclosure. For respiratory distress, open the mouth and make sure that the glottis is clear of debris. Consult a veterinarian.
Respiratory System: Glottis and trachea	Frothy saliva; open-mouth breathing; elevated head; clicking, popping or wheezing noises	Respiratory infection	Increase the temperature of the enclosure. For respiratory distress, open the mouth and make sure that the glottis is clear of debris. Consult a veterinarian.
Neurological System: Behavior and Posture	Improper tongue flicking; gazing; lying on back or side; dull reactions	Meningitis; encephalitis; excess heat; bacteria; viruses; tumors; trauma; amoebic protozoans	Immediately quarantine the snake due to possible IBD infection. Overheating, usually to temperatures in excess of 100° F for more than a few hours, can cause neurological symptoms. Trauma is usually evident. Consult a veterinarian for treatment.
Skin	Excess dried and adhered skin with peeling edges that will not come off	Retained shed	Prevention is the best treatment. Mist the cage while the snake is opaque. If this does not work, provide a sweater box full of moist spaghnum moss (shed box), or soak snake in a 10-gallon aquarium with moistened bath towels and loose cover. Loosen small pieces of skin with high-quality hand lotion applied one or two times each day.
	Crusty, flaking, and often elevated lesions	Fungal lesions	Make sure you do not confuse fungal and bacterial lesions, because treatment is very different. The lesions may require a fungal culture to verify their cause. Treat mild fungal lesions with daily applications of a diluted betadine solution.

Anatomical Region	Symptoms	Common Cause	Treatment
Skin, Cont.	Elevated scales with small protuberances	Ticks	Remove ticks by grasping them with tweezers and steadily pulling them out. If the bite is infected, consult a veterinarian. Watch for more ticks.
	Defined areas of dry, sunken scales	Bacterial dermatitis; mite infestation	Apply antibiotic ointment to dermatitis daily for two to three weeks. Severe lesions may require systemic antibiotic treatment. If mites are present, conduct a comprehensive mite treatment. Consult a veterinarian if problems persist.
	Enlarged, fluid-filled scales; discolored scales; shrunken, crumpled, ulcerated, and reddish-brown scales	Necrotic Dermatitis	This condition is a serious disease, indicative of immune suppression and a concurrent bacteremia. Increase the temperature of the enclosure, and use newspaper substrate. Consult a veterinarian. In mild cases, apply antibacterial ointment daily.
	Soft, fluctuant masses	Aberrant, migrating tapeworms	The mass could be an abscess, though most abscesses are firm. Lance the area between the scales and remove the worms with tweezers. Flush the area with diluted nolvasan, betadine, or peroxide, and pack it with antibiotic ointment daily for five to seven days. Treat snake for tapeworms.
	Firm skin masses	Abscesses; cysts; granulomas; tumors	See a veterinarian for diagnosis (a needle biopsy is one of the best methods). Treatment often consists of surgical removal or lancing.

Anatomical Region	Symptoms	Common Cause	Treatment
Body	Not gaining weight despite good appetite	Parasites, IBD	Have a fecal exam performed, or have passed parasites identified. Treat parasitism as suggested in "Parasitism" section.
	Rear third of body is distended; lack of appetite	If female, it is likely gravid; if male, it may be constipation, or fluid retention secondary to systemic disease	For females, follow directions listed in Breeding Columbian Boas. For constipation, see below.
	Firm mass within the body; possible bloating	Constipation with balls of uric acid and retained fecal masses; in females, it may be retained fetal matter	Soak constipated snakes in tepid water for one or two hours each day to encourage defecation. Exercise should accompany soakings. If problems persist, consult a veterinarian, who may perform an x-ray or ultrasound.
Muscles/Bones	Small, solid lumps attached to the ribs; firm, bridged areas of the vertebral column	Calcified ribs; calcified vertebrae; discospondylitis	Calcium and fibrous tissue deposits build up on injured ribs to repair and strengthen them. Injured vertebrae are often bridged together by calcium and fibrous tissue deposits during healing. Discospondylitis represents and area of bone that has become secondary to trauma or bacteremia. Consult a veterinarian for significant or painful lesions.
	Fused, distorted vertebral column	Osteitis deformans; bone infections (osteomyelitis)	The cause of progressive bone disease is unknown, though some think it is due to a virus. Osteomyelitis can be secondary to IBD, and quarantine is prudent. Though treatment is possible, the prognosis is poor.

Anatomical Region	Symptoms	Common Cause	Treatment
Cloacal	Red, moist tissue bulging from cloaca (vent)	Rectal Prolapse	Make sure to differentiate this between abscesses, granulomas, and tumors. Moisten tissue with a moist compress or bandage, Vaseline, or petroleum-based ointment (Neosporin or Polysporin), and take the snake to a veterinarian, who will replace the tissues and add restraining sutures. Excessively dry rectal tissues die and require surgical removal.
Gastrointestinal System	Regurgitation	Overeating; inadequate heat; gastroenteritis; IBD; foreign bodies; protozoal or fungal growth	Reptile literature suggests that IBD is a common cause of regurgitation, but I have found that it is a rare symptom of IBD, though the possibility warrants consideration. In overeating cases, make sure the snake is well hydrated, and check the cage temperature. Stop feeding for several days, then resume it with small prey items. Treat fungal growth with oral doses of nyastin at 100,000 units per treatment. For protozoal growth, see "Parasitism."
	Bloody, mucus-laden, or rancid stools	Gastroenteritis; parasites	Rule out the possibility of parasites, and treat as regurgitation (above).
Hemipene	Tubular, reddish mass protruding from the cloaca	Prolapsed hemipene (males)	If the prolapse is recent, gently clean the hemipene, lubricate it with a petroleum-based ointment, and replace it. If problem persists, consult a veterinarian. The prolapsed hemipene may require amputation.

Anatomical Region	Symptoms	Common Cause	Treatment
Tail	Hard, dry, crusty tail tips; swollen, raw, and bleeding tail	Retained shed	Moisten retained shed with antibiotic ointment until you can gently lift and remove retained layers. Temporarily bandage raw and bleeding tips. Exposed bone at the tip of the tail requires surgical removal. Some cases may require systemic antibiotics. Carefully monitor subsequent sheds, and provide a shed box.

Typical Signs of IBD in Boas and Pythons

	Acute Phase	Chronic Phase
Boas	Lethargic Apathetic demeanor Lack of appetite	Secondary bacterial Infections Non-healing wounds Central Nervous System (CNS) lesions Mild head tremors Gazing Lack of equilibrium Tremors/seizures
Pythons	Gazing Lack of equilibrium Tremors/seizures Lack of appetite Apathetic demeanor Respiratory infections Sudden death Inability to control movement Signs of CNS distress	Death Severe signs of CNS Chronic respiratory infections in some Burmese pythons

INDEX

selecting your boa, 29–31